Conversations With Money

by

Richard W. Friesen

Published by Themis Press https://themispress.com

https://conversations.money/
First Edition: January 2022

ISBN 978-0-9838199-8-1 (Paperback)
ISBN 978-1-0879-8955-6 (Ebook)

Contents

Foreword

Money is not the most important thing in life, but it's right up there with oxygen.

~ Les Brown

Creating a positive and productive relationship with money will impact your life more thoroughly than almost anything else you can do.

After almost thirty years working with hundreds of clients as a business and relationship coach, it is my experience that a person's relationship with money mirrors their relationship with life itself. When my clients clean up how they think about money—what it means to them; what role it plays in their lives; how they go about earning, spending, saving, and investing it—this not only empowers them to create a wealthy life of unending opportunities, but it also deepens their experience of meaning and fulfillment. Although money won't bring you happiness, if you know how to use it, it can certainly be the vehicle that drives you to find it.

If you want to up-level your relationship with money into something that empowers and inspires you to live a great life, my friend and colleague Richard Friesen is the person you want to talk to. Over the last twenty-five years of me knowing and working with Rich, he has impressed me again and again with his insights into how to use money to enhance human thriving. Whether we were having conversations about the software and algorithms that he built for trading stocks and options, the mindset he taught his traders so they could make clutch trading decisions under pressure, or the contagious delight he exuded when discussing what it means to add value to a transaction, I have always profited from hearing Rich's perspective.

When he told me that he was writing this book, *Conversations with Money*, I thought it was a clever idea. Rather than just talk about money, get into dialog with it! I imagined that it would be entertaining and helpful. It turned out to be so much more than that. This book took me on a profound journey that guided me to rethink my fundamental ideas about what money is, what role it plays in my life and in society, and how it can increase my ability to contribute to the world. The more I got caught up in the story, the more insights I had about how I talk about money, how I feel about money (or the lack thereof), and the role that money plays in my experience of satisfaction and fulfillment in life.

There are thousands of books about money that teach you techniques for saving or investing or earning it. There are hundreds more that tell you what you should think about money in order to become abundant or wealthy. This book is not a treatise like the others; it is a story. It is an adventure! As you follow the main character through his experiences, the book gently confronts you with your own beliefs about money, then systematically guides you step-by-step to transform and enrich those beliefs. This book is not just a collection of ideas that you are supposed to agree with; it is a series of experiences and exercises that open up new possibilities for you.

If you want to transform your relationship with money such that you unleash your creativity and productivity; if you want to work in concert with the world such that you provide value and receive value in return; if you want to better your life, the lives of the people you care about, and the entire world, then this book is meant for you. Richard Friesen delivers on his promise to take you on a journey that will forever change your relationship with money—for the better.

— Mark Michael Lewis,
Founder of the Human Thriving Institute

Acknowledgments

Writing the acknowledgements is challenging, because there are so many collaborators who helped me at every stage of production. The contributions are now mixed into the final results, creating magic that could only happen with each contributor's honesty and heartfelt feedback.

Personal Support

Firstly, I appreciate the personal support from my wife, Marty, who supported my last four years off and on with frequent encouragement and uninterrupted space and time. My assistant, Lindsay Cohen, does everything I can't do. Also, I give thanks to my coaching clients and group members, whose growth and development have been nothing short of inspiring.

Major Contributors

David Robb took a copy that looked like a movie script and changed it into a story, adding richness and depth to the character Julie. This shifted the feel of the book from a Socratic dialogue into a rich and compelling tale.

Next, I'd like to thank the contributors who have had a major hand in shaping the final draft. First, Scott Adams, *Dilbert* cartoonist and author of *Win Bigly*, gave the original draft two thumbs down. His critique inspired a new format that delivers the concepts more effectively. Karin Wiberg had the most challenging job of editing an early version that was almost too rough to edit. However, thanks to her help in shaping the earlier draft, we had something to build on. A. K. Wood ruthlessly cut out thirty percent of the book that was mired in the minutiae of conversation, so the significant points could shine. She also helped transform the feedback from our early readers into improved language and communication. Robin Fuller was engaged to do the final proofreading but contributed so much more. By putting herself in the story she improved the impact not only on herself but for our readers.

Personal and Theoretical Inspiration

My intellectual foundations rest on so many wonderful and inspiring people. Carl Buchheit from NLP Marin gave me the structure of human expansion and growth. Michele Masters and her Money Magic course contributed to the exercises. Peter Connor, co-leader of my Mind Muscles Academy mastermind group, helped shape the concept of "context" as a way of understanding repeated behaviors that no longer serve us.

Intellectual Frameworks

The concepts in this book were inspired by a broad range of authors and thinkers. The following rise above the crowd:

- Walter Williams identified money as "Certificates of Appreciation"

- L. Michael Hall, for his focus on clear thinking and communication

- Fritz Perls, who laid the foundation for my training at the Gestalt Institute
- Byron Katie, who simply asked four questions
- Peter Ralston taught me the value of "Not Knowing"
- Alfred Korzybski simply said, "The map is not the territory."
- Ayn Rand, who wrote the most potent "money speech"
- Thomas Sowell's personal story and free-market support
- John Enright from the Gestalt Institute and Good Neighbor Project
- Scott Adams reframes the world and focuses on process, not outcomes
- Jordan Peterson and his clarity on the human condition and culture
- Carl Buchheit, who humanized neuro-linguistic programming
- Robert Leppo, who is my model for courage as a speculator
- Ray Dalio, who explains economics in simple human terms

Volunteer Army of Editors and Reviewers

I am fortunate enough to have a fantastic community of contributors who believe in making the world a better place. Each of these people made a difference at different stages of the book. I had so many early readers that this list is not complete.

Adrian Li, Albert Lau, Ann McGlinn, Colleen McClure, Danny Csavossy, David Hawthorne, David Kohler, Dean Wolf, Denise Buckel, Don Ramer, Ed Hannan, Emily Penner, Eric Ho, Erton Muhametaj, Gary Burdick, Gary Craig, Glenn Osborne, Gregory Nelson, Hana Radar, James Kelly, Jameson Rikel, Jeff Stearns,

Jenny West, John Jensen, John Ullman, Kristen Stone, Laura Millington, Mandeep Gill, Michael Diaz, Michael Filighera, Michelle Burdick Michelle Hurlbut, MJ Wetherhead, Natalia Holmes, Raji Raman, Richard Wills, Robert Rutter, Ryan Sharp, Tammy Southwick, Wofgang Linder

Engagement Exercises

This book contains several exercises that invite you to explore your unique approach to money and wealth. The goal of the exercises is to expand your awareness, assist you in accepting your discoveries, give you a new menu of choices that support your values, help you feel better, and get you to your goals. I encourage you to take this opportunity for self-discovery.

You can read detailed instructions for the exercises in our complimentary online course. Learn more and register here: https://conversations.money

Introduction

It was the dead of the night, and I awoke with a start. I heard a clear, deep voice say, "You are only worth two hundred thousand dollars a year."

The hair still stands up on the back of my neck when I recall that night. I sat up in bed. It was 3:00 am. My wife was sleeping peacefully. No one else was in the room, and the only explanation was that the voice came from deep inside of me. The powerful tone of the voice made clear that it was not to be questioned.

Without wasting another second, I climbed out of bed, showered, dressed, and drove across the Golden Gate Bridge to the Pacific Stock Exchange in San Francisco, where I made my living as an independent options market maker. I got to the exchange floor so early that the doors were still locked. When the exchange staff opened the building, I went to the deserted trading pit and stood where I always did, at the outer edge. Then I gazed at the most advantageous trading spot, between the two busiest brokers and right in front of the exchange's order book official. In this spot, a trader could clearly hear what was going on and have the first crack at orders. However, this spot was always held by the most aggressive and toughest risk-taker on the floor.

"You are only worth two hundred thousand dollars a year."

The voice from the middle of the night came back—but I realized it no longer applied to me. I walked to the very front of the pit, planted myself in the coveted center spot, and waited for trading to start. The other market makers began drifting in a few minutes before the 6:30 a.m. opening bell. No one seemed to give any thought to my new position, except for the guy who considered it his rightful territory. He stood beside me and started making small talk, but kept one eye on the clock. Right before the bell went off, he tried to nudge me aside.

I didn't move.

An electric jolt went through the pit, and everyone took a step back as a shoving match ensued. I got the upper hand by imagining I was wearing concrete boots. The order book official quickly warned us to break it up or receive a ten-thousand-dollar fine.

I was still in "the spot."

The bell went off, and I became a wild animal. I was screaming, waving my hands, buying and selling as fast as I could write tickets. The other market makers and brokers surely thought that Rich Friesen had lost his mind.

Over the next two months, the pit finally conceded that the spot was mine.

That year, I went on to make many times my previous limit. It turned out I had an internal limiting thermostat that was set by my beliefs about worthiness. The voice I'd heard in the middle of the night represented that limit. Once the voice of unworthiness expressed that belief so clearly and succinctly, I realized that it didn't apply to me anymore.

I used that year's profits to build my own independent trading firm. Some of the traders I hired used my low-risk trading strategy and made money from day one. Others struggled week after week, and no amount of additional knowledge or training could help. It soon became apparent that some of these traders were trapped by their own internal limitations. Upon exploration, I found that their conflicts were similar to mine—and produced the same result.

I'd heard a voice in the middle of the night that triggered significant new beliefs and behaviors. That transformation came out of the blue. From that point on, I was fascinated by the possibility of taking that "accidental" voice and the resulting positive changes I'd experienced and turning them into explosive progress—*intentionally*. Was it possible to create viable, lasting internal change that would improve the lives of the people I worked with and cared about, as well as the lives of good-hearted people in the world at large?

This book is your invitation to engage directly with "Joe," a struggling journalist who is barely making ends meet, as he opens his eyes to the internal beliefs and behaviors that keep him from living the life he wants. A character who calls himself Money pays Joe an unexpected visit, kicking off a relationship based in the desire to uncover Joe's deepest beliefs about personal wealth. By joining Joe and Money in their dialogue, you'll discover powerful ways to reframe your own beliefs and behaviors around money, wealth, and success. Dropping into the conversations between Money, Joe, and Joe's love interest, Julie, will be educational and inspiring in and of itself. Engaging in the suggested exercises throughout the book will help you internalize the joy and freedom of your revitalized relationship with money.

Additionally, you can join our online community and take the Conversations with Money course. Here you'll discover your roadblocks, identify the positive intentions driving costly repeated behaviors, and step into a new context where positive, life-affirming behaviors feel better to you, helping you honor your values and reach your goals.

I have reviewed more than two thousand assessments from people who feel limited by their financial boundaries. My private coaching clients discover that fixing broken economic beliefs not only changes what's on their bank statements, it makes a positive impact in the rest of their lives. My live online meetings have touched hundreds of people, from wealthy money managers and entrepreneurs to people from every walk of life who are struggling to make ends meet.

I've learned that many good-hearted students and clients are frustrated with the conflicts between their values and their financial goals. Our world continuously puts out very mixed messages about success, wealth, and money. We all want to belong, so we reshape our most profound values to fit in, creating a struggle to achieve financial peace.

I wrote this book to address the pain and strife resulting from economic, political, and personal financial beliefs that don't serve us. I've learned that the limitations I faced were not poured in concrete, but simply scripts in my head. If we change our beliefs, we can change the world. We don't need magic, manifestation, or vision boards with exotic goals if we simply step into rapport with ourselves and our ability to deliver value to others.

Through my professional training and life experience, and stories from hundreds of clients and students, I've learned that issues with money are not the real problem, but a symptom, stemming from deeper beliefs about the world and ourselves. As a result, Money and Joe start their conversations by building a solid foundation not only for a money-positive life, but for all aspects of a fulfilling life in terms of work, relationships, and meaning. I invite you to be patient with Joe as he undergoes the deeper changes that make a better relationship with money possible.

After you read this book, you will not look at your relationship with money the same way. You may ask, "Will I make the same transformation that Joe does?" This book is about how Joe expands his menu of life choices and takes charge, or agency, of his own life. You are your own agent, and you have options every step of the way. I invite you to expand your menu of life choices with every page you turn.

Open this book and step inside Joe's head as he wrestles with the very solutions he most desperately needs. Fight for him every step of the way, so that each of Joe's revelations becomes your own.

Joe is about to put his bank card into the ATM. You can join him now...

Chapter 1 — The Email Scam

Standing on the sidewalk near the intersection of California and Van Ness, Joe Everie felt the usual twinge of apprehension as he inserted his debit card into the ATM. A brisk afternoon wind off the Pacific was cutting through the Golden Gate Bridge, and the temperature was dropping by the second. Joe couldn't be bothered with the fact that he'd left home without a jacket. The physical shivers combined with his worry only raised his anxiety. All of his attention was on the ATM screen.

Don't be ridiculous, he told himself, knowing that the payment for his most recent article was supposed to have been deposited automatically yesterday. *You have plenty of funds.* Joe entered his PIN. Yep: the money was there. He let out his breath—unaware he'd been holding it—and withdrew twenty bucks. He liked getting paid for writing, which was his passion. On sleepless nights, he wondered if "passion" should really be driving his career... but the thought of slogging through a nine-to-five job quickly strangled such thoughts.

Sometimes, a publication's payables department would delay his payment by as much as sixty days. This happened often, even though he had been selling freelance articles for almost a decade. Only recently had he started to make a name for himself in the social justice beat. Thinking about how much power these publications had over him always ticked him off. Not wanting to go down that rabbit hole today, he quickly pocketed the cash. As usual, the message on the ATM screen made him grimace: Do you want a receipt?

"I don't want a receipt. I want money!" Joe said, louder than he meant to, as he ended the transaction. "Screw you, and your damned injustice—and I'll say it to your face!" Turning, he saw the woman behind him hurriedly step back to give him a wide berth.

Five minutes later and two blocks away, Joe stepped into his favorite deli. The place was slightly over budget, but it did have its perks. The food was delicious, the crowd had an authentic feel, and the wait was never long. Best of all, the young woman working behind the counter had caught Joe's eye about six sandwiches ago. Joe found her attractive, of course, but it wasn't just that. There was something about her voice and the smooth, unhurried way she moved that gave him a little jolt every time he saw her. He hadn't built up the courage to ask her out, but he knew her name was Julie, and she knew he was Joe... so there was that, at least.

"Hi, Joe," Julie said when he reached the counter.

"Chicken salad sandwich and a large black coffee, please," he said a bit too loudly. Julie gave him a smile that made his stomach flip-flop as she set about preparing his order. Joe enjoyed watching her work. She seemed to turn even the simple task of preparing a sandwich into a display of grace. All too soon, she bagged the order, took the crisp twenty-dollar bill Joe had pulled from the ATM a few minutes ago, and handed him his change. "Thanks for another great sandwich," he said, dropping two dollars in the tip jar.

Sitting on a bench and shivering slightly in the ocean breeze, Joe ate lunch in the small concrete park nearby, oblivious to the passing traffic and pedestrians. How long would it be before he thought of something clever to say to Julie? And how many sandwiches would he have to buy before he worked up the nerve to say it?

A little later, Joe walked up the sagging stairs, unlocked the double deadbolt, and entered his studio apartment, determined to do what he always did when he got home: grab a soda, kick off his shoes, and drop into the office chair he'd rescued from the sidewalk. His throne of creation was indeed a zone for thinking, writing, and wasting time. His laptop—a MacBook Air that was no longer state of the art—struggled to boot up. The hard drive made cranky grinding noises as he swiveled nonchalantly in his patched-up chair. When it finally quieted down, he followed a few hashtags on Twitter, got a little depressed, laughed at a few jokes, got depressed again, swore he'd spend less time on social media, checked another hashtag, then logged into his email. The first message looked like spam—until he saw that it mentioned his blog.

From: Money <money@conversations.money>
To: Joe Everie <JoeEverie@gmail.com>
Subject: Interview for publication

Dear Mr. Everie,

I see that you write for several social and political magazines and have a good following on your blog. That's no small accomplishment these days. However, I feel strongly that your writing about money is clichéd and promotes beliefs that don't serve your readers well. As a qualified expert on the topic of money, I am offering my services to you.

So how about this: let's have a few conversations about the philosophy and psychology of money, and the cultural models whizzing around in your head. What's in it for you?

Everything. (In fact, this stuff is so important, it's going to be the basis for your first book.)

I'll contact you again to set up a meeting. In the meantime, mull over what money means to you.

Sincerely,

Money

As a published writer, Joe had an inbox full of spam—but this was way more personal than the usual ilk. The signature was arrogant, and the presumptiveness was annoying. Who the heck would start a conversation this way? A troll? An old friend playing a lame joke...? Or maybe it was a life coach, all too happy to offer him a free twenty-minute session, then upsell him on a long-term coaching package. He started to trash the message, then hesitated. Perhaps it had something to do with the boldness of the approach. Maybe it was an unacknowledged desire to see what would come next, and the fact that he was always on the hunt for a good story to tell.

He left the message in his inbox unanswered.

After a couple more hours of writing, fidgeting, and rewriting a tricky article for Themis Publications that was due soon, he ate his mac and cheese dinner straight out of the pot. As he speared the last bite, a loud banging filled the room. Joe let out an involuntary squeal, and the fork flew across the room. It took him a moment to realize it was a fist pounding on the door.

"Mr. Everie... Mr. Everie! You can't ignore us anymore. Mr. Everie, come to the door."

Joe's startle reflex was immediately replaced with panic. He knew what was about to happen. He had shut out the problem for so long that now the built-up pressure was exploding on the other side of his door.

Joe remained frozen until the pounding stopped. Then he saw the manila envelope as it slipped through the sizable crack under the door. Joe stayed frozen in primal defense, just like his mammalian ancestors had been programmed to do. Then he pointedly ignored the envelope and went to bed, pushing the grim reality of his situation out of his mind.

Chapter 2 — The Scream and the Reply

J oe threw off his blanket and pushed himself up onto his elbows, breathing hard, aware that he had just screamed loud enough to jolt himself awake. He sat up in the dark bedroom, throat constricted, body shaking. He forced a deep breath, relieved to be free of the nightmare. He couldn't remember all the details, but the panic he'd felt in the dream clung to him like a heavy wet blanket. The lingering vivid image that had triggered the scream was one of Joe crawling on the floor in a crowded public place, trying to scoop up stray coins while people walking by stepped on his hands. He had watched helplessly as his fingers disappeared, one knuckle at a time.

Unable to go back to sleep, Joe got up and turned on the lights. After a few minutes of staring at the lid of his closed laptop, he decided to take another pass at the article for Themis Publications, the online media and magazine arm of an economic research organization. Though he had already coaxed out a passable first draft, he knew it was far from done. Still shaken by the dream, he swiveled his chair from his desk to the kitchen, started a pot of coffee, and promptly spilled half a bag of grounds on the floor. Ignoring the mess, he opened his laptop and listened to the hard drive grind away as it slowly booted up. Sitting down with mug in hand and gritty coffee between his toes, he considered how to make the most of the article for Themis. Writing for this outlet gave Joe valuable exposure, which occasionally led to other work and funneled a stream of fresh subscribers to his blog.

However, for all Ian's social warrior credentials, the editor-in-chief at Themis ran both hot and cold. He was either quick to use words like "talented" and "standout" when reviewing Joe's work, or to fly into a rage loaded with personal insults. Joe wanted to live up to the former and dreaded the latter—even more so when the lousy pay was late.

Ian had once revealed his core fear to Joe when commenting on one of his articles. "There is never enough, Joe—never enough to escape the hammer's drop."

He stared at the article on his screen. It was a long-form piece about the growing divide between the very wealthy and the very poor. Something was missing, but Joe couldn't put his finger on what. At a loss, he searched through his Google Drive, eager to review the statistics and articles he'd saved during the weeks spent researching and outlining this piece.

Among the materials were transcripts of interviews he'd recorded with people in dire financial straits. Joe reread a conversation with Alice, a mother of three young children who was facing eviction. Her husband was in the final stages of his struggle with leukemia. As Joe's eyes moved down the page, he felt the blood rush to his face and his pulse quicken, though he hadn't moved an inch. How could a landlord with a home in San Francisco, two SUVs, and a boat anchored in Tiburon be so damned heartless?

Joe opened a new document and began to type, the anger pouring like acid from his fingers into the keyboard. His thoughts came so quickly he could barely keep up. The phrase "left behind" repeated itself in his head—and on the page. His grammar checker suggested corrections, but he ignored them. The repeating phrase and the idea of poor people doomed to live a life of fear and hopelessness seemed to fuel his frenzy.

Writing about Alice and her delinquent rent payments was easy. But when it came time to write about the wealthy side of the economic divide, Joe's fingers stiffened on the keyboard after typing some well-worn clichés. He understood Alice's dilemma well enough, but how much did he know about the people so far removed from Alice? His familiarity with the wealthy came mainly from movies and television. Sure, he'd met a couple of fat cats at parties thrown by a college friend who'd done very well in the start-up world... but those people were all arrogant jerks who showed up with costly wines to establish their status for anyone dim enough not to know.

As Joe stared at the blinking cursor, the *ding* of a new email interrupted his thoughts.

From: Money <money@conversations.money>
To: Joe Everie <JoeEverie@gmail.com>
Subject: Upcoming conversation
Dear Joe,

I know how passionate you feel about these financial issues. Your writing speaks volumes, but maybe it's time for some thoughtful considerations.

Are you ready for our first conversation?

—Money

He calls himself "Money?" As if! Probably a scammer running a con... Joe began to craft the perfect snarky reply in his head, but his musings were interrupted by a familiar ringtone. He stared at his phone, finger hovering over the red End Call button.

To alleviate his guilt after moving so far from Akron, Ohio, and seldom being able to afford flying back for a visit, Joe made an effort to talk to his mother once a week. Guilt won out. With a resigned sigh, he clicked the green button. "Mom?"

"Hi, Joe. I just wanted to let you know that Mr. Johnson died."

"... Who's Mr. Johnson?"

"The man who lived down the street. You know, the one with the three dogs and that awful little white car with the bad tailpipe."

Joe hardly remembered the guy, but he knew his mom was rattled, or she wouldn't have called. He let her talk for a bit, then gave her his condolences.

"Your father's here. Why don't you say hello?"

Before Joe could reply, his mom wordlessly handed the phone over. He heard the inevitable rustle and sigh of his dad taking the receiver. Though their conversations were few and far between, Mike Everie never failed to begin them all the same way: "Hey, son, how ya doin'? Got a good job yet?"

Joe's eyes were drawn to the manila envelope still halfway under the door. "Did you read that article I wrote? I sent the link."

There was a long pause, but Joe already knew what his dad was going to say.

"Yeah, yeah, I got it... How much did it pay?"

"Not much, Dad. But I get by."

"I have a friend who moved to Frisco. He's a successful consultant and has a lot of connections with some of the corporations there. Call him and have lunch—see what opportunities might come."

"Dad, it's 'San Francisco,' not 'Frisco,' and I'm not ready for a corporate job." *A lot of good a corporate job did you... Even your pension fund didn't survive.* As much as he wanted to say this, Joe bit his tongue. He sensed that his dad had left the room, leaving his mother holding the phone. Joe quickly said goodbye and hung up.

When he returned to his computer, another email from Money was waiting in his inbox. This time, it triggered the same whirlwind of feelings he experienced every time he spoke to his dad. Rather than deleting the email, Joe hammered out an angry reply, not even bothering to correct typos.

From: Joe Everie <JoeEverie@gmail.com>
To: Money <money@conversations.money>
Subject: Interview for publication

jerk you dont know anything about my financial condition...Stop your weird shit. You are a psycho and a moron. I'm blocking you.

BTW calling yourself Money is a stupid gimmick. Who does your marketing? Your high school sister?

Chapter 3 — The Two Dates - The Awesome and the Awful

T he next morning, Joe hit the snooze button three times. It was the thought of visiting the deli later and seeing Julie—even if it was just for five minutes, with a counter between them—that finally gave him the energy to roll out of bed. After his usual shower and shave, he picked out a well-worn pair of casual slacks and a polo shirt instead of his usual jeans and T-shirt. Ready to start the day, he sat too quickly in his office chair, and the back wheel slipped out of the bracket as he struggled to stay upright. Swearing a string of curses, he turned the chair upside down and pushed the defiant wheel back into its slot.

Hoping for something good as he opened the article he'd been working on, he read the first sentence. Maybe it wasn't as bad as he feared.

Five minutes later, Joe knew he was right: it was *worse* than he feared, long strings of uninspired words fraught with ideological detours lacking any direction. After struggling for a few hours more, he decided to trade his battered chair and laptop for some fresh air, anticipating a chicken salad sandwich and dreading his appointment with the editor of Themis at the same time. Maybe his luck would change, and Ian would be in his rare effusive mood.

On his way out, he noticed the manila envelope still on the floor. As if it were a snake, he walked delicately around it.

As Joe approached the deli, he appreciated its strategic location, on a busy corner near a transit stop and convenient to upwardly mobile young professionals, as well as to the boho crowd who rented the surrounding studio apartments and aging rent-controlled flats. Stepping up to the counter, he caught Julie's eye.

"Your usual, right? Chicken salad on rye with a large coffee to go?"

Joe shrugged and prayed he wasn't blushing. "It's a good sandwich."

Julie grinned and bent to the mundane task of preparing his order. All too soon, she was finished. "That'll be seven eighty-five."

Joe pulled out the leftover ten-dollar bill from his previous visit. "I was hoping you were working today. I was hoping... uh... wondering if maybe... you, uh..." Joe paused. He wasn't accustomed to being tongue-tied, but something about Julie left him at a loss for words.

She stared at him expectantly, eyes narrowed.

"Do you have a straw?" Joe blurted out. "Or maybe a stir stick?"

Julie grabbed a straw and wooden stir stick from behind the counter, but stopped short of offering them to him. "Is this really what you want?" She paused, holding the items just out of Joe's reach. "...Or maybe you meant to ask for my phone number instead?"

Joe's ears turned red as he opened his mouth for a moment before saying, "Option B."

"Are you sure?"

"Definitely."

"Give me your phone and I'll text it to you."

The twelve blocks between the deli and the Themis office were notoriously sketchy, even at midday. Joe usually kept a vigilant awareness of his surroundings and avoided eye contact at all costs. Today, however, he practically bounced there, high on the fact that not only did he have Julie's phone number, but dinner was in the cards—for tomorrow night, no less, and at his favorite Irish pub.

Joe mentally reviewed the articles he'd written for the publication, whose mission was research into the effects of economic policy. Given their more progressive and enlightened views, he was surprised to note that their support mainly came from very successful tech industry leaders. He had carved out a niche for himself by focusing on the life of "the little guy," the working-class person who lived paycheck to paycheck—the people who struggled as he did. Mostly, the articles mixed advice with personal stories, so the reader could empathize with someone who worked hard or had bad luck. They couldn't save for a rainy day or put a kid through college, no matter how hard they tried. What was the secret to staying out of poverty, let alone getting ahead financially? *Was* there really a secret —or was it systemic, as everyone assumed? And if the system was rigged, was it even possible to get out of the money trap?

Joe felt the weight of these thoughts as he recalled the email from the troll who called himself "Money." Money's arrogance only increased his irritation.

Joe soon reached the aging building that held his editor's office. Taking the familiar slow elevator up to the fourth floor, he made his way to a small reception area. There was no receptionist on duty, as usual, so he knocked politely on Ian's door before entering.

Ian slowly glanced up from a desk strewn with papers, books, and a laptop framed with sticky notes. Without acknowledging Joe, he just started talking, like they were in the middle of a conversation.

"Joe, you have to bring me something fresh. Frankly, your recent articles all sound the same."

"... I'm fine, thanks for asking."

"Oh, sorry, I, uh..."

"Well," Joe sputtered, saving Ian from his loss of words, "I'm working on the growing gap between rich and poor, and the shrinking middle class. Everyone senses this, but I'm putting a face to it. Every story has a real-life example, up close and in full color."

"That's what you always do. Change it up a little. Run down the data that supports the broader picture of how outcomes are systemic and unfair."

Joe sighed. "I have interviews that support the stats, but if data is all you want, I can get more."

"No, it's not *all* I want. Don't bring me rows of mind-numbing numbers, Joe. Make it come alive."

Ian returned to his computer. Joe stood there awkwardly, unsure what to do with this mixed message. "Okay, Ian," he finally said, "you'll get new pages next week."

The editor burst into laughter, amused at something on his screen.

Joe worked late into the night, digging for new data. He ignored a flurry of emails from the con artist/life coach/practical joker who called himself "Money" and was itching for some face-to-face time with Joe. Whether Money simply got his kicks from annoying people or was going for a more extended con didn't matter. To make matters worse, he was pretty sure that he'd been followed home from Themis that day. He'd noticed a well-dressed man—at least, he assumed it was a man, given that the stranger stuck close to the buildings and seemed to stay in shadow—walking half a block behind him. He stopped when Joe stopped and picked up the pace when

Joe did, causing Joe's animal instincts to go into overdrive. He cut through the tiny urban park, reached the far side, and whirled, ready to face down the stranger—but the guy was nowhere in sight. Getting tailed was an unusual occurrence in his neighborhood, but it wasn't unheard of; people who looked like they might be profitable easy pickings sometimes got followed home. But the truly bizarre thing about today's short-lived drama was that Joe wasn't really a good target.

After yet another email from Money popped up in his inbox, Joe blocked the sender's address with righteous satisfaction. It counted as an accomplishment. Content that he'd never hear from Money again, he closed his laptop and crawled into bed. Then he remembered the envelope under his door. He struggled with himself, but finally got up and brought it back to bed. His heart sank. Sixty days, it said. Sixty days...

He let the letter marked Notice to Appear fall to the floor and pushed aside all thoughts of work. Instead, he fantasized about Julie and mulled over possible topics of conversation for tomorrow's date night.

Chapter 4 — The Nightmare Emerges

"Joe? Wake up, Joe... Yoo-hoo?!... Joe!"

Joe's eyes popped open, and he bolted upright in bed, desperate to scream, but his voice failed him. He was immediately aware that he had been followed home. The well-dressed stranger from the street was sitting comfortably in Joe's battered office chair, one long leg gracefully crossed over his knee, his face hidden in the dark.

"Gee, I must like you, Joe, 'cause I don't 'yoo-hoo' for just anyone."

"Who are you, and what do you want?" Joe squeaked out the words through his constricted throat.

The stranger shifted a little, moving into a patch of weak light spilling through the window. Joe stopped breathing, every hair on his body standing on end. The uninvited visitor was human-like—his proportions were human, but his features were hard to focus on because his eyes, nose, and mouth were perpetually shimmering.

Finally, Joe's voice matched the terror he felt with a guttural scream.

"Joe! Relax, Joe! I'm not here to hurt you. Quite the opposite."

"Jesus Christ!"

"No, I'm not Jesus Christ."

Joe put his hand on his nightstand. His fingers brushed against his phone—a move not lost on the seated intruder, despite the darkness.

"Don't do that. You called me, remember?"

"What do you mean, I called you?"

"At the ATM a few days ago, when you couldn't bear to look at the receipt."

Joe's jaw dropped. "Were you watching me?"

"First, you called me—and then you ignored my emails."

"Oh, I get it... this is a dream. I'm still dreaming!"

"Truth be told, Joe, you have been dreaming for an awfully long time. But at this moment, you are one hundred percent wide awake.

"I know you've been having nightmares about money—you and almost everyone else who is financially conflicted. So I thought an email would be an easy way to introduce myself."

"I asked for *money*, not a hallucination in the middle of the night!"

"Exactly: you asked for money. So here I am."

"You can't be money! Money has no personality. Money isn't real."

The stranger opened his mouth to speak, but Joe cut him off. "You know what I mean."

"I can take a lot of forms, Joe, but this is the one I thought you might be most comfortable with."

Joe buried his face in his hands, as if that might help. "I don't care if you are money. Get out!"

"Millions of people want more of me. They plead, and beg, and curse, and threaten, and try to entice me every single day. But I chose *you*. Don't you want to know why?"

Joe just stared at the stranger, fearful and confused.

"You're the perfect storm, Joe. First, you harbor misconceptions about money that reflect the wider beliefs of your culture. Second, you genuinely care about people and making the world a better place. Third, you both despise money, and want more at the same time. And as a bonus, you're a good writer."

"I don't despise money!"

"Oh, really? I've read your articles."

"They aren't even about money; they are about fairness!" Suddenly realizing he was arguing with his own hallucination, Joe shouted, "Shut up, Joe! Just shut up! Stop talking to this imaginary... whatever it is."

The stranger maintained eye contact with Joe, waiting for him to finish his fit. Joe closed his eyes and kept them shut for what felt like an eternity.

When he opened them, Money was still calmly sitting in the chair.

Joe sighed. "Alright, what are you going to do to me, so that I can get you to go?"

Money threw back his head and laughed. "I'm not going to do anything *to* you. We're just going to have some conversations. See, most people hold limiting beliefs that create the same financial struggles over and over again." Money glanced at the open envelope Joe had left on the table, which wasn't lost on Joe. "Your species has made great strides in technology, health, and communications, but your relationship with money has started to go backward. I very much want a better relationship—not only with you, Joe, but with your friends, your communities, and the world at large. And the key isn't just a practical financial education, but the beliefs that underlie your relationship with..." Money paused for effect. "... me."

31

"I don't want a practical financial education and stay out of my beliefs. If you really are who you say you are, just shit a giant pile of cash and go!"

Money stifled a chuckle. "I'm not going to defecate anything, because that wouldn't solve your real problem. On the one hand, you despise wealth—and on the other hand, you want more. You're out of rapport with yourself and fighting your own mind."

"I am not fighting my own mind. I know my mind. I am fighting you!"

"Many lottery winners spend all their winnings and end up right back where they started, if not someplace worse. It's not money; it's beliefs. We can examine the beliefs and behaviors holding you back from a good relationship with me in an honest conversation. I want this for you, and as a gift to your readers."

"You're going to tell me the secrets of making money?" Joe asked flatly, waiting for the next step in the expected con.

"No, Joe, no list of secrets. I know you have a lot of questions. Just know that I respect who you are and what you believe. We'll steer the direction of our conversations together. Everything we discuss will be carefully examined and aimed at identifying and improving your core beliefs, one step at a time. I hope that as you expand your thinking, you can write about your experience. You do have talent, you know."

"Oh, I get it. You want me to be a ghostwriter for your crazy ideas. That's funny—a ghostwriter for a real ghost! I can see the title now: *The Five Secrets of Getting Rich, from the Money Ghost*."

"Charming, Joe. We're going to talk about all the ways our relationship is screwed up. *By reframing how you think about me and your understanding of money, you will see me through a new lens that reflects your value as a person and the values you hold.*

"Ultimately, you'll weigh all the perspectives and integrate them or discard them. You'll especially become aware of the mechanisms you use to keep yourself poor, and how to adopt new behaviors that support your goals and values."

"What do you mean, I keep myself poor?! Are you trying to tell me that I'm *choosing* to be poor? That sounds like some sort of conservative crap—that the poor are poor because they lack moral fortitude."

"Most of the choices people make are based on unconscious beliefs. These driving forces often come from early experiences. As you bring your beliefs into your awareness, you will be able to make choices that work better for you and others."

"So, just tell me what choices to make and be done with it."

"There are dozens of books about making more money. They sit on the shelves of thousands of readers who are still struggling. *Our conversation is about our behaviors, beliefs, and even how we see ourselves. Your mindset is the foundation for making money.*"

"Like *Think and Grow Rich* nonsense?"

"Joe, that was an amazing book for its time in history. Napoleon Hill and I had great discussions while he wrote. And now it's your turn for a wake-up call. We're going far deeper, Joe. We are going to look at what drives your thinking."

Joe remained silent as he considered his life—or better put, his lack thereof. He thought about how angry he felt, how frustrated he was with the system and his lack of progress. He felt his repulsion towards money, and his resentment of those who had it. He considered his options, including telling this ghost to go to hell and never come back. But he knew Money was touching on a fundamental truth. Still, giving in would be an abdication of control, and Joe hated to give up control.

Suddenly, a new thought popped into his head that patched over his concerns. *I'm a journalist—and this is one hell of a story! Besides, Ian said he wanted something new, so what is there to lose?*

"What are you going to do next?" Joe asked. "Do I get more ghost-mails, or are you going to keep popping up and scaring the shit out of me?"

"I know how to contact you. I'll be back when you're ready. See you soon." With that, Money faded from sight just as Joe noticed the sun rising outside his window, like a scene from a vampire movie, crashing through his confusion.

Joe wanted to get up, brew a cup of coffee, and jot down everything that had just happened. Then a wave of fatigue washed over him... fatigue unlike anything he'd ever experienced. Too tired to think or move, he collapsed back into bed and fell into a fitful sleep.

Chapter 5 — The Techies in Their Teslas, and the Homeless in Their Tents

T he stop-and-start hum of traffic, the rattle of skateboards over concrete, and the shouts of pedestrians—sometimes playful, sometimes otherwise—filtered in through the single-pane windows overlooking the street. This was the way every weekday started... and the reason Joe couldn't sleep. He wrote best when things were quiet, so he often worked late into the night. The price was waking up exhausted just as the rest of the world was going to work.

Based on the sounds outside, the 874,000 people who called San Francisco home were having a typical morning. Joe's morning, however, was anything but typical; it was a pivotal point in his life. Either Money was real, or he had detoured straight into Crazyville, with no idea how to reroute his mental GPS. Joe had never faced such an alarming dilemma. So, he did the only thing that made logical sense: quarantined the night's experience in an emotional lockbox and moved on, as if it had never happened.

After spending more time than usual cleaning up a week's worth of accumulated trash, dirty dishes, and spilled coffee grounds, he flopped into his patched-up chair and plowed into the article for

Themis. Focusing was a challenge, but Joe refused to call it quits, even though he could barely restrain himself from logging off early and heading to the deli to meet Julie.

He arrived at five thirty on the dot, wearing an outfit his mother had sent him two birthdays ago: nice slacks and a still-new button-down shirt. Waiting at a table in the far corner, Julie stood up when he entered. Her cross-body bag matched her knee-length dress, and her hair was long and loose, her natural curls dancing as she crossed the room and playfully shook his hand.

"Hello, Joe Everie. Pleased to finally meet you properly."

"Hey, you look great," he said.

"You clean up pretty well yourself," Julie said with a smile.

After a short walk, they entered a lamplit pub, cool and dark and empty at this time of day. They were quickly seated at a corner table in the back. Julie ordered the lamb stew, and Joe opted for his go-to dish: bangers and mash, with a pint of Guinness.

Julie glanced around, taking in the dark wood paneling, oversized leather booths, and timeworn Irish memorabilia. "Geez, this is like being in another era."

"I think that's why I like it."

"Well, we're the youngest people in here, and the whole design is—"

"Are you originally from the city?" Joe interrupted, feeling defensive.

"I grew up in Indiana and came here for college. After two years slogging it out in general studies, I put school on hold—mostly on account of how much I had to borrow. Taking out so much money when I had no idea what I wanted to do with my life was a terrible idea... one I'm still paying for, by the way."

"I take it the sandwich shop isn't a career, then?"

Julie shook her head. "Just a stopping point on the way to one. Mei—she owns the place—Mei forgets more about business on her worst day than many people know on their best. I'm learning a lot about what it takes to not only start a business from the ground up, but to keep it running in the black."

"So, what kind of business do you want to own one day?"

Julie's eyes narrowed. She looked at Joe for a moment, debating whether she wanted to answer. Then she laughed suddenly, shook her head, and changed the subject. "I know you're a journalist, but what does that mean? Who do you write for, and what do you cover?"

"I'm freelance—mostly social justice articles with an economic focus. One of the publications I write for is critical of capitalism, so most of the articles they commission are about the flaws in our economic system and better ways to organize our politics—stuff like the upper one percent not paying their fair share, how there is no safety net at the bottom, and how big companies exploit their workers. The piece I'm working on now is about how the rich keep getting richer while the poor keep getting poorer. And San Francisco is—"

"Crazy expensive?"

"A great place to live if you want to write about this stuff." Joe paused, feeling the weight of his words.

"What's the article's title?"

"The techies in their Teslas, and the homeless in their tents."

Julie repeated the rhythmic phrase, moving her body like a rapper. "The techies in their Teslas, and the homeless in their tents!' You do have a way with words, Joe Everie. I will give you that."

Joe laughed nervously. "That's just a working title. Ian—one of the editors I work with—always changes my titles, but I keep suggesting them anyway."

"So, techies in their Teslas,.." Julie paused with a mischievous grin. "...virtue signaling while driving past the homeless?" Julie giggle at her own humor.

Joe's face jerked up as he met Julie's steady gaze. At that moment, the memory of his nighttime conversation with Money broke free of quarantine and hit him like a brick. "Well, what should be done, you see... The thing is, the system is rigged to limit wealth to the..."

He trailed off as he noticed Julie's expression shifting. She leaned back, staring at him without a response.

Joe covered his comment quickly. "I haven't written the conclusion yet." He smiled. "But I should have the final definitive answer in a couple of days."

Julie seemed to understand she couldn't push him any further, but her sparkle dimmed at the same time.

Just then, the food arrived, and awkwardness hung over the pair like a San Francisco fog as they ate. The rest of the evening was spent in light conversation about movies they liked and bands they loved.

But something was missing, and Joe knew it.

Chapter 6 — Do You Know What You Want?

"**H**ey, Joe, let's go for a walk."

Joe jumped up from his desk, an involuntary sweep of his arm knocking his can of soda to the floor. It rolled noisily to a stop at Money's feet.

"I convinced myself you were a dream, because the alternative is that I'm crazy,"

Joe whispered. "You can't be real... you *can't* be."

"So let's just *pretend* I'm real. Can you do that, so we can move forward?"

"On one condition: I'll pretend you're real, but you have to warn me before you materialize."

Money responded with a soft chuckle. "How about I warn you by crinkling a crisp hundred-dollar bill?"

The sixty-day notice came to mind immediately. Joe threw a dish towel over his spilled soda, muttering as he wiped it up. "I could use a hundred-dollar bill right now... or even two."

"Excellent start to this conversation. Let's walk and talk about that, shall we?"

"Will other people be able to see you?"

"The astute ones will, like on any crowded street—and if they do, I'll look like any ordinary Joe."

"... GI or six-pack?"

"Glad to see you still have a sense of humor."

"Well, it's better than looking like I'm talking to myself and ending up on the funny farm..." Joe paused with a slight smile. "Even if that's where I do in fact belong."

"Come on, Joe. I even dressed for the occasion." Money gestured at his expensive jeans and Tevas, then flipped up the hood of his hoodie, his face half hidden in shadow. "Very tech-bro, no?"

Joe snorted and grimaced.

A block from Joe's apartment, Money turned down a quiet side street, broad and traffic-free. It bore a charming name and had recently gone through a massive cleanup effort to make the neighborhood more hospitable to small businesses. When they reached a point where no one was within earshot, Joe launched into the conversation without looking at his companion. "You said we were going to talk about the core issues in making money."

"Not quite: core issues in your *relationship* with money." Money let this hang in the air.

"Okay," Joe said a long moment later, "this is the part where you talk."

"Of course. Our conversations will evolve as needed, and will probably wander from topic to topic. But whatever the topic, I'll point to basic principles that will not only impact your money-making ability, but which will invite you to have a more positive experience of your world."

"I didn't ask for a philosophy lesson, or a therapist. I just want everyone to have a fair share."

"You asked for money, and at the same time, you hate yourself for wanting it. Can you honestly expect to receive more money while holding that conflict inside of you?"

Joe rolled his eyes. "How about just sending your advice in an email?"

"That would be easy, but not nearly as effective. What do you want, Joe? Let me be more specific: if you could ask for anything, what would it be?"

"Anything? Asking for anything is a sucker's game that's been around for generations. When I was younger, I prayed for things that were important to me. I prayed for my mom to be happy, for my dad to notice me, for my parents to be in love again. I even prayed that Kenny, the playground bully, would find somebody else to pick on. Trust me, he didn't."

"What are you saying, Joe?"

"You can't fool me twice."

"Do you think just being aware of what you want means magically having your request fulfilled? Our inquiry will focus on clarifying your deepest desires, so you can begin to hear the conflicting voices in your head that are waging war on one another."

"I'm not at war with myself! I'm at war with the world and everything in it... or more precisely, the world is at war with *me*."

"So, what would you like instead of being the person the entire world keeps picking on?"

"I want enough money to pay my bills." Joe's mind involuntarily called up the image of the stapled documents inside the manila envelope with the court date. "I want to quit being pushed around by my publishers and live a better life. I want to live in a world that is fair to everyone. I don't even want to *think* about money. Is that too much to ask?"

"You can ask for anything—and that's a good start." Money paused. "Are you aware of how angry you sounded as you asked for this?"

"Damn right, I..." Joe bit his lip, and his voice trailed off. "I'm pissed off," he said as they left the alley and turned onto one of San Francisco's busiest streets. He was too caught up in the conversation to care if anyone was watching them.

"So, having money—what would that do for you?"

"What would money *do* for me? Are you kidding? You *are* money —and now you have the gall to ask what money would do for me? Now it's *you* that's pissing me off!"

Money allowed a long silence to pass between them. When he finally spoke, he measured his words. "I'm going to get tough now, Joe. I care about you, and I believe you can handle what I'm going to say."

Joe gritted his teeth, a bad habit left over from adolescence. "Do I have a choice?"

"You *always* have a choice with me. The best way your life will improve is by you making choices based on beliefs and behaviors that are aligned with reality. *Anything that you yourself haven't worked through and experienced positively will not be helpful.*"

"How about rather than making me a better person, you just make me a richer person? Give me a lot of yourself! Now that would solve the problem!"

Money sighed softly. "Okay, let's play it your way. First, sit down on this bench so we can play an imagination game. Are you good with that?"

Joe moved toward a bench facing a small park and plopped down, signifying half-hearted acquiescence.

Money sat beside him. "Now, close your eyes to reduce distractions. First, notice what's going on physically. Start with the top of your head and work down through your body, and tell me what you notice."

"What has this got to do with money?"

"Are you afraid to notice your physical sensations?"

"Of course not. But..."

"Joe, I honor every aspect of you. As you bring more awareness to your physical sensations, emotions, and thoughts, we can honor those parts of you and listen to what they say. We'll be doing more of that later."

"Oh, no. Not this woo-woo crap..."

"It may be a little 'woo-woo,' but it isn't crap. So, tell me, what do you notice?"

Joe closed his eyes. "I am noticing that I don't want to notice."

"Excellent. Now move that awareness to your face."

Joe took his time while his thoughts distracted him. "The first thing I notice is that my face is all tense. I wasn't aware of it until now, but I am clenching and unclenching my jaw."

"Good start. Bring that awareness to the rest of your body and tell me what you feel."

"I feel the wood slats under my rear. I notice my breathing is shallow, and my chest is tight. This conversation is making me nervous, and I feel butterflies in my stomach. One knee is bouncing up and down, and my other leg feels tense." Joe paused, surprised at the many sensations, a realization not lost on Money.

"It is what it is, Joe. And that's okay. This awareness isn't meant to create a judgment, but to invite curiosity about your present state of being. So, for now, please accept what you noticed. Allow it to be as is, without judgment."

"All my life, I've motivated myself with self-judgments to make sure I keep pushing. If I stop judging myself, what will push me forward?"

"... And how is that working for you?"

Joe's jaw clenched; however, it was with awareness this time. He crossed his arms over his chest in silence.

"We just touched on one of the core issues: expanding your self-awareness. The next step is accepting what you learn about yourself. These two shifts—expanding your real-time awareness and accepting what you discover—are the first two doors of the Golden Keys. More on that later; let's go back to the original question. Having lots of money: what would that do for you?"

"I could stop worrying every moment of every day about how to pay my rent, buy groceries, pay taxes, and everything else. Once I take care of my bills, then I can do the things I want to do." Joe paused and started laughing. "And I could tell everyone what I really thought! I would quit being polite to assholes."

"So, what you want, Joe, is to stop worrying and speak your mind?"

"I don't want to just stop worrying. I mean, I could take drugs if I just wanted to stop worrying. What I want is to solve the cause of my worry."

"So, the cause of your worry is lack of money?"

"Damn right! Not just for me, but for the disadvantaged all over the world."

"So, rich people don't worry?"

"Sure, they worry—but they have more amusing things to worry about! 'Should I drive my Tesla or my Ferrari today? Should I buy a mansion on the ocean, or in the mountains?'"

"So, what you want is a better relationship with money?"

"I don't want a *relationship* with money! I want fairness!"

"Do you think that's possible?"

Joe remained silent and rubbed his scalp, as if to erase his doubt. "I don't know."

"What you are ignoring right now is my relationship with you."

"Your relationship with me? What relationship with me? You don't have a relationship with me."

"That may be truer than you know."

Joe wavered, not sure how to respond.

"Would you like to discover for yourself my relationship with you?"

Joe wavered again, unable to put his thoughts into words as a mental fog took over.

Money put a reassuring hand on his shoulder. "It's time to introduce the first exercise, which will let you see Joe through *my* eyes."

"Look here, Mr. Money, I only agreed to a conversation with you. You said I could take what I wanted and leave what I didn't. You keep stretching our agreement. I'm not doing any exercises."

"Yes, I understand how the thought of doing exercises creates a feeling of exposure, and even vulnerability. However, the door is open for you to step past that feeling and experience a foundational awareness. This exercise is important if your new book is going to be effective."

Joe felt his chest tighten instantly. "Whoa there! First there were conversations, then the imagination game and some exercises. Now I need to write a book?" Joe stood up, reflecting his agitation.

"This is a good time to check your physical sensations." Joe opened his mouth to argue but stopped himself and paused with a deeper breath. "You *are* a writer, aren't you, Joe? And you do want more money, and to be able to help others with their own financial suffering? What if stepping into a simulation would help you discover how you hold yourself back from your own financial success?"

Joe crossed his arms, sat back down, and pushed himself back in the seat, expressing his recalcitrant attitude. "How bad is it?"

"The exercise is another imagination game. And when we're done, you can write down the results, so you can use them for your book."

Joe's face softened. "You won't hurt me, will you?"

"I promise I will never hurt you, but you may feel some discomfort."

Joe took a deep breath, and the exhale caught in his throat. He remained silent while his thoughts, fears, and hopes for a better life created a cacophony of confusion in his head. "Okay, Money," he finally said, "you've made an offer I can't refuse."

Three Chairs Exercise — Your Relationship with Money

Issue: Some of our beliefs and attitudes about money can be outside of our awareness. These hidden attitudes impact our financial success, health and even our well-being by altering our behaviors and how others react to us.

Exercise Description: You will create three voices that speak for different parts of yourself, and you will sit in a different chair to speak as each voice. First, you speak as yourself and talk to money about your experience with it. Next, you discover how money sees and reacts to you and your current issues. Finally, you step into your wisest self, who distills insights from the interaction. Each voice is given time to speak and be understood.

Outcome: With the increased clarity and wisdom gained from each voice's perspective, you can bring acceptance to all your parts. As you build internal rapport, you can then ask, "What would I prefer?"

Time to Complete: The exercise will take from thirty to sixty minutes.

Prerequisites: A guide who will read you the instructions

Exercise Access: You can find detailed instructions in your complimentary online course.

Join or log into your complimentary online course here:

https://conversations.money/book-exercises/

Chapter 7 — Joe Becomes Money

Without speaking, Money pulled two chairs from the scuffed bistro table in Joe's kitchen and put them beside the desk chair, arranging them so they all faced each other. "Each of these three chairs represents a unique voice," he said. "This first chair is you as you are now. The second chair is money. Not me—just money itself."

"And the third chair?"

"That's for an independent and neutral observer." Money pointed to the first of the kitchen chairs. "We're ready for you to step into this exercise. Please sit in chair number one. This is the easy part; you'll just be yourself."

Joe nodded and sat down on the edge of the chair.

"Next, let's fill chair number two with money. What vividly represents money to you? Physical cash? A bag of gold? Bank statements...?"

"You've got to be kidding. Here you are, the living incarnation of money, asking me what *I* think represents money?"

Money nodded. "We want a better idea of *your* beliefs."

"Geez... I guess a pile of cash would work."

Money passed in front of the chair opposite Joe—and in that instant, the chair was filled with a big pile of hundred-dollar bills, neatly bundled and neatly stacked.

Joe blinked, stunned. "Is that real money?"

"It is. In fact, it's enough money to let you live for twenty years or more with no financial worries."

"How much?"

"Five million. So, as you look at those five million dollars, what do you notice in your body? What are your physical sensations?"

Joe paused to survey his body. "I have butterflies in my stomach, my breath is short, and I just want to grab it."

"Excellent observation. Now, how do you feel emotionally?"

"I feel excited and eager to be so close to the money. I want to grab it and have all my dreams come true. I feel hopeful... uh..." Joe paused.

" 'Uh,' what?"

Joe didn't respond.

"What thoughts are going through your head, sitting so close to that much money?"

"Thoughts? They're more like fantasies of what I would do with all that money. Another thought: 'Do I get to keep it?' Oh, and another thought just whizzed by: 'Is this the devil's way of tempting me? All this evil money, and I almost fell for it.'"

"Good. Now, let yourself expand those feelings. Notice the excitement you're feeling, the butterflies in your stomach, and the fantasies and dreams. And also, notice the judgments. I'll give you a moment." Money paused.

Joe shook his head, not in reluctance, but in surprise. "I feel like a demolition derby is going on in my head and body. My feelings and thoughts are crashing into each other."

"Good. Now we're going to amplify that experience. I want you to do everything you can to feel what you're feeling even more intensely."

Joe stared at the pile of money in chair number two. He started to shift and squirm.

"On a scale of one to ten, how intense is what you're feeling right now?"

"I'd say I am already up to a seven. That much money in one place is both awesome and painfully intense—and even evil and seductive!"

"What do you want to name that pile of money?"

"Uh... the obvious, I guess: Abundance."

"Now I want you to tell Abundance what you think about it. Don't worry about me being here. I won't take it personally."

Joe glanced at Money with the expression of someone riding a roller coaster. He turned to Abundance and stared intently. His face became flushed as his breathing became more rapid and shallow.

"Joe, tell the money—"

Joe cut in. "Abundance, you're so close to me; you are right in front of me. Why can't I have more of you?" His voice tightened. "You could do so much for me. You could make my life so wonderful..." His voice trailed off. "But you're just *sitting* there! I'm pissed off at you. Yes, that's right: I'm pissed off!"

"Excellent, Joe. It's important to hear that voice. Now, sit back for a moment, and check for other voices that want to say something while you're looking at Abundance. Allow any voices to emerge that want to be heard."

"There's something there, but... it seems kind of gray and fuzzy."

"Keep looking at the money, take all the time you need, and invite those voices to bubble up."

"The pissed-off voice is so angry that it scares me. I don't want to let it out."

"Sometimes our angry feelings are like a boiler that's ready to explode. Giving the feelings a voice can feel dangerous. Does that seem right?"

"Yeah... I don't want to go there."

"I have no plan for you, nor do I need you to change. However, this voice you've pushed down has something important to tell you. Can you allow that voice to be heard?"

"I may not have a choice." Joe's voice shifted lower. "I feel this anger is unstoppable, like having to vomit."

"May I have a conversation with that angry voice?"

"I think that train has already left the station, so go ahead."

"Does this angry voice have a name?"

" 'Pissed.' That's the name."

"Thank you, Joe. I'm now going to talk to Pissed." Money made a show of clearing his throat. "Well, Pissed, Joe has permitted me to talk to you. I understand you're pretty angry. I also believe that you're an important voice for Joe, and that you have a valuable message. To be clear, I'm not here to get rid of you. I want to understand you better and listen to the message you have for Joe. With that understanding, would it be okay for us to talk?"

Joe leaned back in his chair, closed his eyes, and remained silent.

Money leaned forward. "Pissed, can you hear me?"

Joe responded in a gruff tone that Money hadn't heard before, throaty and loaded with emotional energy as it spoke one word at a time. "I... am... not... in... the... mood... for... conversation."

"For this moment, be as angry as you want. What do you want to tell Abundance?"

Joe's voice tightened as the pissed-off voice reacted to Abundance. "I'm angry at myself for wanting you—and I'm angry at you for all the evil money creates. It's people with money that cause the most pain and suffering in the world. That's why it feels so good to deny your right to exist." His words came faster and faster, his pitch rising. "I should be happy without you, but I'm so weak, I want you anyway. I want to be rich myself—and at the same time, I hate you for all the wealth you've given to assholes who don't deserve it!"

"Thank you, Pissed. I now have a sense of how angry you are, both at yourself and at Abundance. I hear a voice that wants wealth, and a voice that is angry at wealth. Does this seem right?"

"No," Joe responded firmly in his Pissed voice. "I have just one voice. I don't want wealth; I want fairness for Joe and the world. Joe wants wealth when he is weak, but this is a Trojan horse that sneaks in the beliefs we both despise. I keep him angry so that he doesn't get caught up in greed."

"You want fairness?"

Pissed remained silent.

"How do you create fairness?"

"We need to destroy everything that maintains the inequity of privilege."

"And then everything becomes fair?"

The question produced a long pause.

"I've said enough."

"Thank you, Pissed. I appreciate your desire for a better world."

In the silence that followed, Money allowed Joe to feel the intensity of the voice that had overwhelmed him. Neither spoke for several minutes.

"Joe, take a few deep breaths, and when you are ready, come back to me and clarify what just happened."

Joe took his time to shake off the fury that Pissed had exposed. When he did speak, his own voice had returned. "Yeah, sure. Actually, it's a relief to get that out of my system. I had no idea."

"We'll talk about that later. Right now, let's continue the exercise. Now that you are back to me as Joe, take another deep breath and a quick awareness trip through your body."

Joe took a few deep breaths, then paused before he fumbled for words to describe his experience. "Okay, I'm back. I'm Joe again. But that was weird. I mean, geez, it felt like a real part of me had a voice of its own! I mean, like, wow... I mean, uh... it felt like it wasn't me saying those words."

"You did a great job. Are you ready for another voice?"

Although Joe didn't feel like unleashing another torrent, he took a breath and nodded.

"Now, please sit in the chair with Abundance. Wiggle into the pile of money so that it surrounds you."

Joe looked at the pile of money, still shaking off the residue of his anger. "Sit in the chair with all that money?"

Money just nodded. Joe felt an instant shift that electrified his body as he settled into the cash. Several stacks fell on the floor, as if to say there was so much that it just didn't matter. Joe couldn't stop the shit-eating grin that spread over his face.

"Now, let's learn what Abundance has to say about Joe and Pissed. Take all the time you need and feel yourself becoming Abundance. Become those hundred-dollar bills. Slip out of Joe's body, and just become money itself."

As Joe took several slow, deep breaths, a solemn expression replaced the smirk on his face.

Money's voice settled into a hypnotic rhythm. "With each breath, you become less of Joe and more of money. Breathe Abundance in with each breath, and exhale Joe with each breath."

Joe did as told, and his internal state shifted as he felt the power of being money itself.

Sensing this shift, Money said, "Abundance, I want you to look at chair number one, Joe. You know him rather well, so tell me what you notice first. It's important to tell Joe the truth."

Joe's back straightened and his shoulders broadened as Abundance took over his countenance. He gazed softly at the imaginary Joe seated in chair number one. "Joe looks sad. I mean, *really* sad. He looks all alone."

"Good observation, Abundance. How attracted are you to Joe?"

"I want nothing to do with him."

"You also heard from Pissed, Joe's angry voice. What did that part feel like?"

"That's part of the reason I want to move away. Why should I deal with Pissed's crap?"

"What else did you notice?"

"The drama of two voices beating each other up. I have no interest in stepping inside that boxing ring."

"What two voices did you hear?"

"I heard him both wanting me and being intensely angry at me."

"As you look at Joe, what are your physical sensations?"

"I feel kind of sick to my stomach."

Money took a moment to decide what instruction to give next. "Okay, Abundance, move your chair to a place where you feel more comfortable."

Abundance slid his chair backward, and several bundles of hundred-dollar bills fell to the floor. Abundance surveyed the fallen cash before returning his gaze to Money.

"From here, please look at Joe again. What does Joe feel like from *this* distance?"

"This is better. I want to stay out of Joe's reach."

"You sound pretty cautious. Can you tell Joe what that's about?"

"Sure. Joe writes about me like–"

"Talk directly to Joe."

Still surrounded by the remaining cash, Joe picked up a bundle of hundreds, as if to solidify his role as Abundance. He looked squarely at chair number one and the imaginary Joe. "Joe, you write about me like I'm the devil himself. At the same time, when I get close to you, you just grasp at me. The harder you grab me, the less I want to be around you, because you feel so needy."

Money nodded. "Abundance, I appreciate your willingness to experience this exercise fully. I'm going to talk to Joe now. Is there anything you want to say before you go?"

"I've had my say, and I appreciate being listened to."

"Joe, please step out of Abundance's seat. Take a few moments and shake your body around."

Joe stood up, took a deep breath, and shook his limbs while looking back at the money that was now in a chaotic pile.

"Welcome back, Joe," Money said, nodding in approval. His voice lowered and became hypnotically rhythmic again. "Now please go to chair number three and become the wise observer. As you sit in this chair, notice how your observational skills are improving. You feel peaceful and nonjudgmental towards both Joe and Abundance. With each breath, you feel calmer, more confident, and more discerning every moment you remain in that chair."

Breathing deeply, Joe settled into the experience of observing Joe and Abundance. The reality of their relationship brought tears to his cheek.

"As a keen observer of humanity, do you have a name?"

Joe smiled and snorted. "Bonzo."

"Bonzo is the wise observer?" Money had a quizzical look.

"I am Bonzo, the All-Knowing."

Money laughed, not expecting this rapid emotional shift from Joe. "Bonzo the All-Knowing it is. Please tell Joe and Abundance what you observed about their relationship."

"This is so sad. Here you are, Joe, so close to Abundance—and you chase him away. And there you are, Abundance, so close to Joe, and yet you feel repelled by him. Both of you are just repeating this process over and over without resolution. Every morning, Joe, you wake up with the same beliefs and attitudes, and every morning, Abundance reacts the same way. It's no wonder both of you are locked into the same..." Joe's voice trailed off.

Finally, Money broke the silence. "Well done, Bonzo, the wise observer. Now please sit in chair number one and become Joe again."

"... Do I have to?"

"Maybe not." Money laughed.

After a few moments, Joe got up, shook himself off, and sat in chair number one. Without any prompting from Money, he started to talk to the imaginary Abundance in chair number two. "That was weird, but I get it. I want you, and at the same time, I'm angry at those who have so much of you. I can understand why you hold back from me." Joe turned away from the pile of money and looked directly at his mentor, his voice cracking with emotion. "Money, I have no idea what to do."

"This awareness is the start. One path to improving your relationship with money is using the three Golden Keys—and yes, they are made of gold. But these keys are so precious that they're worth more than gold."

"Okay, Money, I'm ready. What are they?"

"We've done enough for today. Sit with your experience and accept your new awareness with curiosity. Your experience is the start of the Golden Keys. We will build on this exercise later."

Chapter 8 — It Wasn't a Walk in the Park

J oe woke up the next morning feeling groggy. His head ached, and his mouth was dry. With the returning awareness of these new parts of himself—Pissed, Abundance, and Bonzo—it felt like he had stepped into a strange new world. Since these parts had found their voice, they wouldn't shut up. "I suppose they'll be poking each other in the eyes next," Joe muttered to himself, remembering the *Three Stooges* movies from when he was a kid. Hoping his internal jabber wouldn't follow him, he grabbed a light jacket and stepped outside.

When he reached the street, an urge to call Julie bubbled up so strongly that it surprised him. Instead, he sent her a text, even though their last date, although pleasant, had left him a little wary.

Beautiful day. Walk in the park later?

A moment later, his phone pinged.

Sure. Swing by the deli at 5:30.

Joe sent her a smiley face, took a quick walk around the block, then returned to his apartment, ready to dive back into the Themis article. All thoughts of Money's exercise vanished from his head as he delved into a world of injustice. By five o'clock, Joe had a rough draft ready for editing, and an unusual feeling of euphoria as he anticipated a walk in the park with Julie.

Joe's phone pinged again.

If you bring a blanket, I'll bring the sandwiches and drinks.

Joe's stomach flipped as he imagined sharing a blanket with Julie. This was even better than expected. He took the fringed throw off the back of his couch—another gift from his mother— and headed out.

They hopped a bus for a short ride to Golden Gate Park, then quickly found the path meandering through the Panhandle and stopped in a grassy area where kids played while their parents watched. Joe pulled the blanket out of his backpack and spread it out.

"Chicken salad, or pastrami and rye?" Julie held out two wrapped sandwiches.

Joe reached for the chicken salad. "Well, if it ain't broke…"

"You said it!" Julie said with a grin, digging into the pastrami and rye.

Their conversation started with easy chitchat, until Julie broached a more serious topic. "How's the article on economic injustice coming?"

"Actually, I just finished the first draft."

"Are you pleased with it?"

"Well, yeah, I suppose… I guess I am."

"You guess?"

Joe laughed nervously. "No, I *am* pleased with it."

"It sounds so much better when you say you're pleased rather than hemming and hawing."

Joe was startled by Julie's directness, which demanded more confidence from him. He always felt apologetic about himself, and he used self-deprecation to make sure he wasn't alienating others. But at that moment, he realized Julie would not play his relationship game; these were new rules.

By the time they'd finished their sandwiches and two bags of kettle chips, Julie knew a lot about the article, the people Joe had interviewed, and the new data he'd found. She pressed him on every point but let up as soon as Joe got defensive.

When she pulled a chocolate chunk cookie from her bag and unwrapped it, ready to share, Joe decided it was time to step out of the spotlight. For a split second, the question that had been consuming him was on the tip of his tongue: *What are your own beliefs about money?* But with his deepest beliefs now a bit shaky, he wasn't ready to open that risky can of worms—at least not yet.

Instead, he asked Julie about the business she hoped to open one day. Julie looked at him for a long moment, the change in her energy palpable. "Design," she said at last. "We spend almost all our lives inside, staring at screens—and when we aren't staring at screens, most of what we see is not only poorly thought out, it's boring."

"I suppose it is boring. I don't really notice. Maybe I'm too much of a veteran screen-starer." Joe noticed defensiveness in his voice.

"Exactly. But that's what I'm here to do: make the world a little more interesting for the people in it. And do it in ways that are affordable, accessible to everyone, and environmentally sound. That's why I'm working for Mai: so much real-world experience."

" 'Real-world' ?"

Julie looked at Joe and opened her mouth, stopped, then laughed. "Yeah, unlike my mom's world. She's trying to help, but sometimes I think she does more harm than good."

"How so?"

"I'm not sure I should tell you."

"Don't, then. I mean, if you're not comfortable—"

"Vision boards!" Julie blurted out.

"What?"

"Every time my birthday rolls around, she sends me a new picture to post on my vision board."

"You mean those corkboards everyone used to decorate?"

Julie nodded, grinning wryly. "Every year, I get new pictures to add. When I was a kid, she didn't give me a puppy, just a vision board with a picture of one. Then it was a trophy when I was on the swim team, followed by pictures of sensible used cars when I went off to college. In the long run, it's a good thing I never manifested a car! Parking in a city like this costs a small fortune."

"Oh, come on! Couldn't you have also manifested the perfect parking spot every time you needed one?"

Julie laughed.

"So, what was the last vision board picture?" Joe asked. "A design studio?"

"I change the vision to be about people who are happy with the value they receive from me. My vision is about delivering value. Then I work back from there to what I need to do. What do I need to know, what skills will help me, what do I need to do every day, and what habits can I build? I also check to see if I believe I can do it. Some days I have doubts, and I check in with them to see what they are trying to tell me."

Julie paused, noticing the furrow on Joe's face. "... Anyhow, my mom continues to vision her own dreams, and I don't try to stop her. It gives her hope. But Joe..." Julie's voice choked. "I want more than a vision of things to *buy*." She stopped and gazed out at the lake, as if she were somewhere far away. "My mom only ever visioned the outcome, not the process or the work involved to get there. She didn't put the pieces in place. She just dreamed."

Feeling desperate to ease Julie's pain, Joe blurted out with agreement. "I want more than a dream, too! I want a world that has a fair outcome for everyone." He realized as he said it that his words sounded too pandering, maybe even phony.

Julie looked at Joe with her lips tightened, but she couldn't restrain her thoughts. "Your articles are doing the same thing as my mom's vision boards." She paused, then slowly but deliberately began to pack up her things. "They envision the outcome, but not the contribution. Your articles are like a vision board for people who don't want to perform."

Joe instantly cringed with embarrassment, but rising anger quickly displaced everything else.

"Joe, I'm sorry. I just..."

Julie's voice trailed off as Joe felt himself retreat behind a familiar barrier to keep his anger from showing.

"Joe, it's okay. What you said about fair outcomes for everyone just hit on a painful... no, not painful. I'll admit it: you hit on something that makes me furious. I want so much more for both my mom and me. I know we can discuss your articles at some point, but they also trigger something..." Julie looked down, took a breath, and looked back at Joe. "I know what just happened. But I can't say it yet. It feels too..."

"Too what?"

"Too intimate to share just yet."

"About your mom?"

"No. About us."

Joe's brain waves exploded with electric intensity on top of his anger. It was like a powerful negative and positive charge hitting him at the same time.

Julie laughed. "I'm sorry. You look like I just hit you with a truck. Look, we have different worldviews, but we both want what's best for everyone. That is a positive intention we share." She paused while noting the look on Joe's face. "I look forward to many creative conversations." She let that sink in. "Can you stay with me and stay connected when we talk about challenges?"

Joe heard her words, but there was no place for them to land amidst the emotional chaos in his head as Julie continued to pack up.

Joe realized he was at a place in his life where two paths diverged. One path was broad, familiar, even comfortable. The other looked like it climbed a craggy, dangerous mountain.

Joe took a deep breath as Julie's eyes returned to his. He looked out across the lake—and thought he saw the familiar figure of Money, wearing a quizzical look. He rubbed his eyes, and the image was gone. But it was enough.

"I can't promise. This is so new." His eyes met Julie's. "But I want to stay connected."

Chapter 9 — The Golden Keys

"**D**o you remember today's agenda?" Money asked.

"The Golden Keys," Joe replied. "Keys to what exactly, I don't know."

Money was sitting comfortably at the kitchen table. Joe offered him a cup of coffee, but Money declined, wanting instead to get right into the day's conversation. "The Golden Keys improve your life by opening your eyes to choices right in front of you," Money continued, "choices that not only feel better, but which honor your values and get you to your goals."

Joe rankled at the mention of "choices," and his attitude was reflected in his voice. "I hoped we were going to talk about the Golden Keys that get me out of the pressure I feel every morning when I think about money—or more accurately, how it feels to not know how I'm going to pay my bills."

"Every time you step closer to your higher self, you'll experience some discomfort. But as we move in that direction, that discomfort will eventually turn into... well, comfort."

"If I stand on a step stool, is that my higher self?"

"Making jokes indicates some nervousness about the topic. The lamer the joke, the more nervous you may be."

"Hardee har har, Money. I don't know that I have a higher self. I just have me... and most of the time, it feels more low than high."

"Being aware of your physical sensations, emotions, and thoughts as they happen in real time is the beginning of connecting with your higher self. With this awareness, you're no longer the experience; you become the part that *notices* the experience, and intentionally gives it the meaning that reflects your deepest values."

"But aren't those automatic reactions the real me—maybe even the *most* real part of me?"

"Yes, indeed. But you're not limited to just experiencing yourself as these temporary emotional swings. You can develop real-time self-awareness, which grows from passive awareness into a higher self-awareness. With practice, this higher awareness starts to possess agency. Agency is the end product of the process of the Golden Keys."

Joe stiffened. " 'Agency'? 'Higher self'? These are magic words that don't mean a thing to me."

"Okay, then look at your direct experience and recall how you, Joe, have made changes that worked better for you in the past. Has there been a time where you made some behavioral changes that worked well for you?"

"I, uh, well... this feels embarrassing. I don't recall a time when I ever intentionally changed my behavior for the better. At least not successfully."

"Can you recall one of those unsuccessful times?"

Joe snorted. "I played the woo-woo game. Yeah, don't tell anyone, but I've made New Year's resolutions. I've talked to myself in the mirror. I've written mantras on sticky notes on my laptop. I took a new-age seminar, gazed at crystals, and howled at the moon. I did a ropes course. I meditated. I fasted. And yet here I am, still struggling with money."

As soon as Joe said these words, he thought about Julie's mom and her vision boards, and how much it upset Julie. A foggy awareness was bubbling up—something about his articles that seemed tied to...

Money interrupted before Joe could explore the thought. "I know you're exaggerating, but still—what a fortune you must have spent!"

Joe nodded glumly. Then the ridiculous irony of the situation struck him. He burst into laughter, and Money joined in.

"Nothing sticks, Money. I lack willpower and discipline."

"I hear the tension in your voice. Is it anguish?"

"Anguish? That's a bit strong... but yes, it's in that direction."

"Great. You've just demonstrated the first Golden Key."

"If that's what the first Golden Key feels like, what's the third— the gate to hell?"

"The first Golden Key is awareness. You're aware of the belief that your solution lies in having more willpower and discipline. With this awareness, we can move on to the next two keys."

"But awareness is so painful!"

"It's not awareness that creates the pain, but the meaning you attach to what you discover."

"I don't understand."

"Imagine an anthropologist discovering an unknown tribe in the Amazon. Imagine them being invited by this tribe to stay and learn their language and customs. Do you think this anthropologist would be judgmental about the amount of clothes they wore, their sexual mores, or the punishments meted out for violating tribal customs? Chances are the anthropologist would be fascinated by everything. It would be an intriguing trip back in time. On the other hand, imagine missionaries from a century ago discovering the same tribe. Their need to reform the tribe would overshadow their openness to learning about our human heritage.

"So, Joe, do you prefer to be fascinated, intrigued, and curious about yourself? Do you welcome every discovery, no matter what it is? If so, there is little pain to be experienced with that mindset. If, on the other hand, every discovery brings a judgment of inadequacy, then it is easy to generate the experience of pain."

Joe's face contorted. "Are you saying that I generate my own pain?"

Money silently held Joe's eyes.

Joe leaned back. "I can't imagine *not* judging myself. I mean, that's how I get motivated." He paused. "And that's not even the worst part; if I didn't judge myself, I might do all sorts of terrible things."

"Is that true?"

"... Probably."

" 'Probably'? Are you one hundred percent certain it's true?"

"I've never asked myself that question before. I've always criticized myself to stay motivated. The very thought of *not* judging myself and still being okay, even getting what I want, has never occurred to me."

"In the three chairs exercise, when you sat in the third chair of the wise observer, did Bonzo have any judgments of either Pissed or Abundance?"

"It didn't feel like there were any judgments. It was just observations."

"Excellent, Joe. You're now using the second Golden Key: Acceptance. The first Golden Key to behavioral change is simply awareness. When that awareness comes with total acceptance, you've unlocked the second Golden Key.

"The third Golden Key is the easiest: Asking. You were joking that the third key is the key to hell, but actually, it's the key to heaven.

Once you're aware and accept your current state of being, all the pressure is off. No more "shoulds," no willpower, and no discipline. You can stop fighting your own brain. You can look with fascination at everything we discover. Without the pressure of judgment, change is simply stepping into new behaviors that feel better in the moment, honoring the values of your higher self, and getting you to your goals."

"But what do I ask for when the world has so many problems?"

"We can simply ask one question: 'What do I want now?'

"So, Joe: what do you want now?"

"I thought I knew, but now I don't know what I want... not now, or tomorrow. I'm drifting."

"How about this: let's draw a map to discover what you want—a map that you'll love."

Being more comfortable with words than pictures, Joe hadn't drawn since he was a kid, but he brightened at the random thought that hit him: *Besides, if I'm a good boy, Money might spring for the box of sixty-eight crayons with the built-in sharpener.* It was one of those small things Joe had always wanted but never got, his mother being of the mindset that no child needed more than twenty-four colors at a time.

But Money was gone, saving Joe the need to explain the humor. Out of habit, he turned to his computer for messages that could distract him from the anxiety of facing more self-awareness. A *ping* announced a new email as the screen lit up.

From: Money <money@conversations.money>
To: Joe Everie <JoeEverie@gmail.com>
Subject: Awareness Exercise

Dear Joe,

Please download the Expanding Your Awareness exercise
and print it out from the online course you can now access.
I look forward to discussing your experience with this
lesson.

—Money

From: Joe Everie <JoeEverie@gmail.com>
To: Money <money@conversations.money>
Subject: Awareness Exercise

You have courses? Online? I feel like you keep dropping
bombs without warning.

—Pissed-off Joe

Overwhelmed by a never-ending onslaught of expanding obligations, Joe hit Send. Agreeing to talk to Money didn't obligate him to
write a book or take courses. Part of him wanted Money to just show
up and rescue him, but all he got was another email.

From: Money <money@conversations.money>
To: Joe Everie <JoeEverie@gmail.com>
Subject: Awareness Exercise

Dear Joe,

Yes, so many things to keep track of that I dropped the ball
by not explaining all of this earlier. If I send instructions in
an email, they get buried and lost. So, I created an online

> course to keep everything in one place. Right now, it's pretty empty, but we can build it out together.
>
> Your username is your email address, and I picked out a password for you. It's the name of the woman you're dating. (You didn't think I knew about that, did you?)
>
> —Money

After a couple of days without another email from Money, Joe realized he was on his own. Still a little put off, he clicked the link to the online course. There he found detailed instructions for the SET (Sensations Emotions Thoughts) awareness exercise. The exercise directed him to set the alarm on his phone to go off every waking hour. As soon as it rang, he would immediately focus his awareness on his sensations, emotions, and thoughts. The instructions told him to score his discoveries on a scale of -5 (totally depressed) to +5 (totally exuberant) and record the results in his online journal.

On the first morning, this is what he recorded:

Conversations with Money: SET Awareness Journal									
Date	Time	Activity	Physical Sensations	Score -5/0/5	Feelings	Score -5/0/5	Thoughts	Score -5/0/5	SET
	8:00 A	Heading to the bathroom	Left knee sore, head feels fuzzy, breathing tight	-3	Feeling excited and uncertainty	3		-4	3.3
	9:00 A	Sitting down to write	tension in shoulders	-2	lost and discouraged.	-2	I need to complete the article or I am shit	-3	2.3
	10:00 A	Writing the article	all good	0	in the flow	0	No thoughts, just flow	0	0.0
	11:00 A	Snacking in cereal	hunger	-2	Anxious	-2	What if Julie doesn't like me	-3	2.3
	Noon	lying in bed	exhausted	-3	numb	-3	This is all screwy. Need to get myself together to see Julie. I don't want her to see me like this. Shit. What do I have to do today. Make the world go away	-4	3.3

Within a day, Joe was fascinated. There was far more going on inside of him than he had ever thought possible, and the data didn't lie. He had never considered himself an unduly negative person, but it quickly became apparent how much time he spent with a tight chest, angry, and criticizing himself.

Expanding Your Awareness
— SET Instructions

Issue: At any moment in time, a treasure trove of information about our physical sensations, our emotional flow, and the thoughts that are coming and going through our heads is available. This amount of real-time information overwhelms the conscious mind, so our brains create mechanisms to reduce the flow. These filters once helped our distant ancestors survive, but now we can open our awareness in real time.

Exercise Description: Setting an alarm alerts you to pay attention to your physical sensations, emotions, and thoughts, catching them raw. Once captured, you will record them in a simple journal.

Outcome: After a few days, your journal will tell a fascinating story about how your internal ecology supports or resists the needed confidence to handle the present reality as it is.

Time to Complete: Intermittent over weeks or months

Prerequisites: None

Exercise Access: You will find detailed instructions in your complimentary online course.

Join or log into your complimentary online course here:
https://conversations.money/book-exercises/

Chapter 10 – Dinner and Debate

T he bus hummed along, the stoplight gods smiling down upon it through a cloudy Saturday night. Joe walked north for a few blocks, arriving at Julie's apartment complex with ten minutes to spare. The building wasn't well kept, but it had a cozy feeling. It was an older complex, and a handful of senior citizens chatted in the courtyard, likely tenants for decades.

Joe texted Julie to let her know he was there. She came down five minutes later, just as a slight drizzle began to fall. Joe called a Lyft, not wanting her to have to walk in the rain. He felt an uneasy pang, knowing the charges for both the car and dinner were going to show up on his credit card. *These conversations with Money certainly aren't helping my income*, he thought. *Why can't Money just shit a big pile of himself and go away?*

While Joe only needed to impress this particular woman, Money wanted to challenge his entire belief system. Despite his internal confusion, a moment of self-awareness washed over Joe. Realizing how tight his stomach felt, he took a series of deep breaths and decided to sit back in the seat and enjoy the Lyft as it took them deeper into Julie's neighborhood.

They entered a bustling Korean restaurant on Clement Street and waited briefly for a table. Once seated, Julie didn't waste any time initiating conversation. She not only asked about his article, but volunteered to read it before Joe sent it to Themis.

Joe felt the earth shift slightly under his feet. Given Julie's persistent questioning, what would she think? The article had just one round of polishing left, and the clock was ticking. He wasn't exactly gung-ho about both satisfying Ian and surviving the sharpness of Julie's review.

An image popped into his head without prompting. During summer camp when he was twelve, he had snuck down to the lake. A canoe was tied to the dock. He put one foot in the canoe. It wobbled. He left the other foot on the dock. Slowly the canoe rotated away from the dock, and Joe realized there was no hope. The further the canoe moved from the dock, the wider his legs spread, and he knew he was doomed to fall. He was due back for a lesson on building a campfire. He arrived dripping wet, leaving no doubt about where he'd been while everyone else was tending their little fires.

Joe had the same stretched-apart feeling sitting in the restaurant. He didn't want to let go of his familiar beliefs on the solid dock, and he didn't want to step into Julie's beliefs that felt like the wobbly canoe. His brain went into hyperdrive trying to find a way to stay out of the water. Instead of committing to sending the article to Julie, he decided to talk about the premise over the food that had just arrived.

"The article looks at the reality of economic disparity as confirmation of the systemic failure of capitalism. For example, what about the single mom without health insurance? What about people who work hard, but are unable to escape poverty? What about racially disparate outcomes... ? These are the tangible results of our current capitalistic system."

"How so?"

"Well, isn't it obvious? You have X system, and you get Y results. If the results are brutal, unfair, and unjust, you have to credit those results back to the system. And if you don't like the results, then you need to change the system."

Julie's eyes drifted away from Joe. She took a bite of the bulgogi she had ordered and chewed slowly. "Or," she said at last, "simply make people perfect. If people were perfect, the system wouldn't matter. Can you create a system where people's imperfections, emotions, greed, narcissism, and hunger for power don't contaminate the system? Maybe, Joe, you're trying to create a system that can never overcome the very tendencies that make us human."

Joe's mind raced. *Where does she get this? She isn't how I imagined her to be when I watched her make all those chicken salad sandwiches!*

But Julie continued without any sign of letting up. "Capitalism is a set of rules for financial transactions. It isn't some sort of evil monster with a will of its own. It was created by imperfect people, and it's organized and run by imperfect politicians. The world is a messy place, and..."

"And what?"

"And we—as individuals—are responsible for our own thoughts and feelings. We're each on our own path, creating our own reality, every moment of every day."

Joe blinked. Could it be that Money was visiting Julie, too? "So," he said slowly, "how long have you held this belief? When did you first start thinking this way?"

"For years and years." Julie's eyes drifted down to her food as her face softened. "I credit my mom, Ardith. I told you about her sending me vision boards. She was big into *The Secret*, before *The Secret* was even a thing. She was ineffective herself, but I learned a lot.

I learned about the power of my beliefs—but more importantly, the power of taking risks and taking action."

"You learned risk-taking from your mom?"

Julie's face sagged as if gravity had just doubled under her chair. "Well, yes, in a perverse way. My mom just..." Joe saw that this was a difficult moment for Julie, and in a surge of wisdom, he remained silent. "... she was stuck with just the fantasy. I swore I wouldn't do that." Her voice took on a strident, defiant quality that Joe hadn't heard before.

"Oh." Joe just nodded in sympathy, not knowing how to respond to such emotional intensity.

"So, I watch my words and my thoughts, and I notice when they aren't positive. If I truly believe that design school is in my future, it will be. My job is to find the pieces to that plan in the real world."

Joe and Julie returned to their food in silence.

Joe took a risk. "And the pieces are at the deli?"

Julie's face snapped up, ready to react, then paused as if deciding whether to attach an insult to the comment or ascribe a positive inquiry. "My problem is that I spend more time thinking than doing." Her face turned red as she said more than intended. "I'm afraid of becoming my mom."

Chapter 11 — Who Wrote the Article?

J oe tossed and turned in bed, his mind busy replaying the kiss he'd shared with Julie before she slid into another Lyft and headed back to her apartment. It was a friendly kiss with a hint of something more, allowing him to fantasize about the future of their relationship. The one thing that gave him pause was how different their beliefs about money were.

Relax, Joe told himself. *How can you judge someone for their opinions when your own are so shaky?*

For the first time in a long while, he felt like he was "adulting." It was a surprisingly comfortable feeling. That night, when he finally drifted off, it was his first night of sound sleep all week.

With the sun streaming in around the edges of the blinds, Joe was surprised to find himself eager to work. He did a few stretches, brewed some coffee, poured a cup, and settled into his chair after pushing the loose wheel back in its place. It took him thirty minutes to read his article for Themis, stopping as critical thoughts popped up in response to every paragraph. When he reached the end, he pushed himself away from the screen, stunned. *Did I really write this?* The words didn't seem like his own. Then, just as he was slipping into dismay, his hourly Awareness Alarm—a cellphone setting so important that he'd elevated it to proper-noun status—went off with a series of beeps.

Joe had started his regular SET check routine when a throbbing pain in the back of his head came to the forefront. He continued to document his physical sensations—a tight chest and hunched shoulders, along with shallow breathing, and wondered: could he be aware of raw physiological sensations without the experience of pain?

Joe sat back and allowed himself to just be with his body. Once there, he realized nothing life-threatening was happening, and he could indeed live with that. With that thought front and center, his breathing deepened, his heart rate slowed, and his muscles relaxed.

Wanting more frequent reminders to access his internal state, he set his Awareness Alarm for fifteen-minute intervals, then scrolled to the top of his article, ready to reread it.

The Economic Collapse is Coming for You!
by Joe Everie

The coming economic collapse is a failure of our capitalistic financial system. The stories I am going to tell are symbolically the canary in the coal mine. These are the stories of the most vulnerable in our society, who are punished by a system that rewards the wealthy, the privileged, and the connected. This collapse will move from destroying the lives of racial minorities, women, and sexual minorities to everyone else.

In other words, it is coming for you. And it can all be avoided—but sadly, it won't be unless all of us demand change.

We are witnessing a dramatic shift in economic disparity, health care, climate, inequality, stagnation, loss of hope, and mass species extinction all at the same time. Obviously, there is one underlying factor driving us over the cliff, and the brakes are missing. No one has the power to stop the car from crashing, which will be the cataclysmic end of humanity and our planet as we now know it.

The predators are in charge. They don't care about the coming collapse. They only care about their greed and consumption, at the expense of everyone else. The problem is that this system is not sustainable. Eventually, the predators will run out of the disadvantaged after chewing them up. Then what? They will look up, notice the game is over, and retreat to their guarded plantations. The rest of us will be left to clean up the mess—not just the environmental mess, but also the social and emotional destruction they have created.

The middle class becomes the lower class. The lower class become the new poor. The poor are abandoned and become casualties. America is the richest country in the world, yet most people do not even have enough money to retire. The average American can't afford to have an emergency costing more than four hundred dollars.

The rich get richer, hoarding the wealth that is meant for us all under a system that could be truly humane and compassionate. But no; this predatory behavior leads by example. The middle class adopts these practices because they don't understand the cause of their pain. Then they turn to the fake solutions of nationalism, right-wing extremism, authoritarianism, and yes, even fascism in a misguided effort to relieve their misunderstood suffering.

Sharon is a single mom raising two wonderfully resilient girls. She lost her job because her boss demanded she work overtime without compensation. She was not able to meet this demand because she needs to care for her children. The stress she experiences daily should not happen to anyone in a nation as wealthy as ours. She can't pay the rent or afford health insurance, and her kids suffer from a lack of healthy fresh food.

Robert, a young man, fell in with a group of kids who felt alienated and banded together to survive. As a result, he was arrested for selling marijuana at seventeen. He is smart, and at the same time, lost. He doesn't see any way out of his hole. A second arrest is now on his record. Unable to get a job, his only option is to go back on the streets. Unfortunately, we have failed to give kids like him the support they need.

Rashawn was fifty-five years old when he lost his middle-management job; a predatory hedge fund had taken over his company. They tore the company apart, fired most of the employees, then sold off the company for scrap at a hefty profit. They produced nothing, yet made tons of money. Rashawn became unemployable. After his wife left him, he was stuck with their debt and two kids ready to leave community college and enroll in a state university. We failed to provide Rashawn the dignity of work and an income. He shot himself at age fifty-seven.

I've interviewed more than a hundred people in the last twelve months, all with stories that leave them little hope for the future. They are all examples of the systemic cancer that is eating away at our society from the roots up. We have wealth, ability, and resources... and yet, the wealthy and powerful hold on to their position, leaving everyone else struggling.

The roots of our economic system are critical to our survival. The financial system we choose from here on out will either nourish these roots or allow them to be ravaged by the privileged. As our resources are consumed and not replaced, there is less and less to go around. The next evolution of this predatory path is fascism, swallowed whole by the gullible. All that the new fascism does is further enforce the predators' rights to continue to rape the world, until there is nothing left.

We have a choice to make that will take great courage.

Are you part of the solution, or part of the problem? Are you blindly marching to the cliff, or do you have the courage to make a better choice?

"The Economic Collapse is Coming for You!" — Analysis

Issue: Language has the power to script a movie in our minds by creating linguistic descriptions, metaphors, and emotional triggers which have easy access to our internal context of beliefs and reactions. Skillfully done, this process sidesteps our rational mind and puts us in a context that no longer has access to analysis.

Exercise Description: In this exercise, you will review Joe's article word by word, issue by issue, you will be invited to think about the critical assumptions embedded in the text.

Outcome: This exercise gives you the ability to pause and use your analytical mind as you gain clarity on the emotional picture Joe creates, and the freedom to discover your own beliefs.

Time to Complete: 1–2 hours

Prerequisites: A careful read of Joe's article, "The Economic Collapse is Coming for You!"

Exercise Access: You will find detailed instructions in your complimentary online course.

Join or log into your complimentary online course here:

https://conversations.money/book-exercises/

Chapter 12 — Joe's Brain Ignites

J oe stopped reading before he hit the added data that Ian had re-quested. He realized he wasn't presenting it as effectively as possible, but that wasn't the issue of concern. Standing, he looked out the dirty window onto the street below. "Who wrote that?" he asked himself out loud.

"Good question."

Joe let out a yelp as he spun around, surprised to find Money bent over his laptop and the open article.

"Who *did* write this article, Joe?"

"Well, my name is in the heading."

"We think about ourselves as a single unified person across time. But we have different voices, as you have discovered, and in different contexts, we draw on different parts of ourselves. Those parts can even create different contexts. Thinking about different parts of ourselves is unnerving. So, if you think about the author as one independent part of yourself, and another independent part of yourself is reading the article—"

"It's Pissed!" Joe blurted out, suddenly thinking of the exercise with three chairs. "Pissed wrote the article."

"Well done, Joe. So, now we have a clear voice that is part of you. Now, listening to that voice, what's the meta-message?"

Joe stared at Money blankly.

"What I mean is, what are the beliefs that create the anger? What world is Pissed coming from that elicits such a response?"

Joe's voice became dark and defensive, as if Pissed had just woken up. "Pissed isn't *creating* this world. He's *describing* it."

"Does everyone else in the world have the same experience as Pissed?"

"Of course not."

"So, there are many interpretations of the same world? Multiple maps of the same reality?"

"This is a trap acknowledging the obvious. Yes, some people may have a different experience. But that's because they're privileged."

"Excellent. Now, what is the positive intention of the article?"

"Caring about fairness. That sums it up. Yeah: I want people to care."

"Pissed, full of anger, wants people to care?"

Joe put his head in his hands and mumbled softly, "Yeah... that's how I get people to care."

"How is that approach working for you?"

"Not so well. I keep screaming at the world, and my voice is lost in all the other screaming."

Money pulled up a chair and invited Joe to sit. "Now that you're aware of how angry Pissed is, you can accept him as he is without judgment, and start to understand the positive intention he has for you and the world." Money watched Joe for a moment, allowing his words to sink in. "You've participated in enough transformational weekends to know that the foundation of caring for others starts with caring for yourself. When that happens, you will then develop a voice that can resonate, be heard, and be effective."

Joe nodded. Caring for himself certainly felt better than berating himself. It was a new feeling—but he had no idea how to let go of the anger.

Money left Joe staring at the screen. As he read the article for what felt like the hundredth time, he was certain Ian would be happy. It hit all the major fear points that brought readers to Themis. Just because it was in Pissed's voice didn't mean it wouldn't resonate. It would resonate easily... with a community of other pissed voices. In a moment of courage, Joe decided to read it once more—but this time with Money's eyes, or at least as best as he could manage.

He poured himself a second cup of coffee, rolled up his sleeves, and dove in—only to be stopped by the first sentence: "The coming economic collapse is a failure of our capitalistic economic system."

Money wouldn't treat this statement like a certainty. He'd probe the belief, wanting to know where it came from and what lurked underneath. If Joe went down this path, the premise of the entire article would change. Softening the language itself with words like *maybe* and *might* would help to some extent, but this approach didn't exactly follow the Themis style guide. Of all the editors at the publication, Ian was well known for attacking "cover your ass" practices.

Joe felt a headache creeping up from the back of his neck, just as his Awareness Alarm went off.

As he mulled over doing another rewrite, his headache intensified. Joe was then struck with an idea to get feedback from Money. He banged out a quick email and included a link to the article in Google Drive. *I think I might need a rewrite. You won't agree with some of this, but I really need some help*, he wrote.

Just as Joe was about to send the email, a new thought flashed across his mind. *Is it Money you're worried about, or Julie?* Joe paused, finger on the mouse button. *What will happen when Julie reads the article? You judged Julie for her take on money, and now you don't want her to judge you for yours. Are you hypocritical, or just human?*

"Screw it," Joe muttered and hit Send.

A minute later, he was pulling a bottle of ibuprofen out of the rusted medicine cabinet with a cracked mirror when he heard the familiar *ding* of an incoming email. Joe returned to his computer, shaking the bottle, happy to hear that a few headache-busting pills were still inside. He bent over the screen, intent on checking Money's reply before heading into the kitchen for a glass of water.

But the email wasn't from Money. It was from Julie.

From: Julie Brubaker <JulieBrubakerDesign@gmail.com>
To: Joe Everie <JoeEverie@gmail.com>
Subject: Re: Can we discuss in person?

Sure, I'll take a look. Why the need for a quick rewrite? And when do you want to meet?

—Julie

Joe bent closer to the screen, not wanting to believe his eyes. Had he sent his SOS to Julie instead of Money? She'd popped into his mind, but had he been distracted enough to make that kind of mistake?

A glance at his sent mail folder confirmed that was precisely what had happened.

Joe put down the bottle of ibuprofen, crossed over to his bed, and fell into it, shutting his eyes. The SET Awareness Alarm on his phone chirped, but he ignored it.

Even through the pain, he heard the *ping* of an incoming text message and knew it had to be Julie.

Joe lifted his phone.

I have an hour before work. Call me.

Joe didn't have the energy or stamina to have Julie analyze the article. But he also knew that not responding after appearing to ask for her input would be a significant rebuff. He tapped her icon, and she answered on the first ring.

"Thanks for sharing the article, Joe. I think I'm getting to know you better because of it."

"Well, I'm not sure why you'd say that, because this article isn't about me. It's about our dire economic situation."

"... Really?"

Joe felt his face flush instantly. That, combined with his pounding headache, left him without resources to suppress his irritation. "It's not about me," he repeated, aware of the tone of his voice. "Julie, I'm sorry if I seem upset. I just have a blinding headache."

"Do you have these headaches often?"

What the hell? Was she probing for medical problems now? Joe paused, realizing that the next few seconds could be critical to their relationship.

"No, this is unusual. I have to have this article in by tomorrow, and well, you see..."

"What's up, Joe? Can I help?"

Joe grabbed a glass of water from the bedside table and took a quick gulp. Why was she willing to help him? Could it be that Julie respected him more than he respected himself? Her response was new and confusing. "I put most of this together with Themis in mind, but only lately realized how angry I was when I wrote it." Feeling a need to come clean, he added, "Frankly, I sent this link to you by mistake. I was afraid that you would feel critical of my beliefs, and that would..."

"Would what, Joe?"

Joe felt his stomach tighten. "Create an argument."

The silence on the phone felt deafening.

After a brief pause, Julie responded. "Given the time crunch, is it even possible for you to rewrite the article? So, take the pressure off yourself, and hand it in as is. I mean, you've written articles like this before."

"Oh?"

"Of course you have," Julie said with a laugh. "I've read them. You think I wouldn't Google what somebody I like a lot has written? This article hardly breaks new ground for you... but I do have a suggestion."

"A suggestion?"

"Rewrite the article—not for publication, but just for yourself. And in every place where somebody is suffering, put your own name."

Joe laughed sarcastically. "So you're saying that this article is simply a projection of mine? You want to be my therapist?"

"No. I don't want to be your therapist. What I want is an honest relationship that is resilient enough to handle who I am and what I think."

The power of the comment hit him hard. But Joe's awareness exercises gave him the ability to be aware of what he felt at this very moment. He could allow Pissed to respond—a move that would undoubtedly end the relationship. Or, he could acknowledge what Julie had just said. For a moment, he felt himself sinking into anger. It took a conscious effort, but he managed to pull himself back. With this shift, he was able to offer a very different response. "I want an honest relationship that is resilient enough to handle everything."

"So, I guess we're on the same page, then," Julie responded cheerily.

They were both silent for some time, and Joe realized Julie's advice was sound. He reviewed the article in his mind during the silence and substituted himself for the victims in his predatory world.

"I think you might be right about the article," he said. "Turning it in as is, I mean."

"Good," Julie said brightly. "Any idea what you'd like to do on our next date?"

Joe was surprised by her response, which seemed incongruent with the tension in the conversation. After a moment, he realized Julie was letting him know she was ready to put the topic of his article behind them and move on. "I have a couple of ideas. I'll see what's available and ping you."

"Hmmm," she said with a laugh, "maybe I'll wear something extra girly and bat my eyelashes for a change of pace."

At that moment, Joe knew that he had found an incredible woman, and that life would never be the same. Everything he believed about the world and himself was now on the table for examination. In that instant, he resigned himself, fully and completely, to a world of both uncertainty and excitement.

Chapter 13 — Keeping Out of the Water

Joe awoke, feeling the remnants of yesterday's headache. His awareness of Pissed's anger in the article and his projection of victimhood was unsettling. Was there another way of thinking? What if his beliefs determined his financial situation? He thought about the three chairs exercise and his own conflicts about money. Would this awareness improve his finances, just like Money promised? Joe corrected this thought as he replayed their many conversations: no, there were no promises. Maybe this was just some motivational poster crap about the journey and not the destination.

With this thought in mind, Joe crawled out of bed and pushed himself through his morning ritual. He locked his apartment door behind him and descended the stairs. It was a bright Indian summer morning, the sky cloudless and blue, a gift for the Bay Area residents. By the time he got to the sandwich shop, his headache had largely disappeared.

Joe loudly drummed his fingers against the counter. A second later, Julie poked her head out of the back.

"What's a guy gotta do to get a little help around here?" Joe asked, dripping with mock impatience.

"It's a little early for a chicken salad sandwich, no?"

Joe laughed. "I'm off to see Ian and thought a cup of coffee might be good for the stroll."

Joe was the only customer, allowing Julie to take her time, drawing a heart on his cup. "An extra girly heart," she said, deadpan, "because I don't feel like batting my eyes."

Joe paid for the coffee and started to put the change in the tip jar.

"Please, no tips, okay? It's strange now that we're dating."

Joe nodded and pocketed the change, concealing the impact of Julie's acknowledgment.

"Joe!" Julie called just as he reached the door. "Whatever Ian says, you'll manage it well. I have faith in you."

Joe was aware of his emotional response as it happened. He turned to the door quickly, without words.

While walking and sipping his coffee, Joe thought about Julie's confidence in him. His brain became a dartboard, with all the darts coming at once: Julie, Money, the systemic failure of free markets, even the three chairs exercise and the voices it conjured up. Lost in the tide of his thoughts, he almost walked past the Rand Building housing his editor's office. He dropped the empty coffee cup in an overflowing sidewalk trash can and stepped toward the building's art deco doors, avoiding a homeless man in a sleeping bag as he did so. Riding the ancient elevator, he checked the folder containing his printout of the article printout and the flash drive with the electronic copy. Then he stepped out of the elevator and turned right. Themis Publications was at the end of the hall, and his stomach tightened as he approached the door.

"Well," Ian said when Joe entered, "I hope you finally have an article for me."

Joe bristled at the implied insult, but simply pulled the copy from his folder and handed it over. He waited a moment, then plopped into the empty chair across the room.

Five minutes later, Ian dropped the copy on his desk and dramatically shook his head. "I wanted meat, not fluff. I want to show exactly how much wealth the rich have stolen from the rest of us. This piece doesn't show that. The numbers you pasted at the end don't reflect the total loss."

"That type of overarching data doesn't exist."

Ian's voice softened. "Our website is seeing a boost in traffic, and we can't waste that. I don't want to lose these eyeballs. We can find a use for this, but I'm not going full rate. I'll give you half rate for it, and you can have another week to get me something better."

"I thought we had an agreement."

"Every piece you've written recently is the same—same language, same issues. Only the headlines are different. It's only a matter of time before people complain, and if they complain online, an advertiser or two could jump ship. Give these people half an excuse to go looking for a greener pasture, and they'll do it. You know that."

Joe struggled with his rising anger, but he needed the money this week for rent, and for the envelope's demand that was due in less than thirty days now. "You've got me over a barrel," he mumbled, "so I'll take it. But this isn't right."

"I'll make it up to you with the next article, if you can get big-picture data and give our readers something they can't forget." Ian reached into his top desk drawer and handed Joe his preprinted check.

Joe tried to slam the door on his way out, but the automatic closing mechanism wouldn't allow him the satisfaction.

"And Joe!" Ian called out after him. "I'm not kidding about next week!"

On the way home, Joe cut across a tiny park. Seeing an empty bench in the warm sun, rare for the city, he sat down to think. On the one hand, Ian had cheated him. On the other, it only confirmed his misgivings about the article's tone and content.

His Awareness Alarm went off at that moment, and Joe noticed residual anger from the meeting. He experimented with accepting the angry feelings rather than subduing them, and he was pleasantly surprised at how quickly they came and went.

If a new type of article was required, Joe was going to deliver. Best of all, he could use his creative skills in a way that would allow him to straddle his conflicting beliefs about money, give Ian the facts he wanted, collect a bigger paycheck, satisfy Money's probing, and impress Julie, all at the same time. The fantasy about fixing everything with one article gave him the optimism he needed. He stayed in the park for fifteen minutes, keeping one foot on the dock and the other in the canoe, at least for the time being.

Chapter 14 — Sources of Suffering

"Hey, Joe. Joe, wake up."

Joe ignored the intrusion and remained on the couch, eyes firmly closed.

"Come on. It's me, Money."

"Good to know it's not Santa Claus. Do you know him?"

"Every fall, he borrows money for toys, but he never pays me back."

Joe laughed and sat up. "Have you read the article?"

"I read all your articles. That is why I chose you, remember?"

"You read all those articles, and you still choose me?"

"I like to think that everything I do has a positive intention for the world."

"Well, I'm positive that choosing me was a big mistake."

"How so?"

"Stop playing games. You read the article."

"It sounds like you're preparing for an argument."

"Can I be honest?"

Money tilted his head. "That's a funny question, given how much we've been through together."

"Julie says the article is a projection of my own crap."

Money pursed his lips.

"Well?" Joe added after a moment.

"Well, what?"

"... Is it?"

"What if it is? What then?"

"Then everything I've believed in and worked for falls apart. Then where am I? What am I left with?"

"This is most excellent! You now have an awareness of both your past and evolving beliefs."

"So, what am I left with?"

"You're left with being a human with a good heart and positive intentions. You are a man who wants the world to be the best place it can possibly be. Can you live with that?"

"Of course I can live with *that*. But then I'm vulnerable to becoming what I hate. It leaves me vulnerable to becoming one of *them*."

"Or, it leaves you vulnerable to finding out who you are without the rhetoric. It leaves you in a place where you can discover who you really are, and the core values you hold."

Joe buried his face in his hands. Without looking up, he spoke quietly. "But what if what I want is bad?"

"Congratulations, Joe. You've brought us to the core of your dilemma."

"You mean what I want to be *is* bad?"

"You know the answer."

"It feels egotistical to say, but what I want from the deepest part of my heart is good. I've always been so afraid of being bad, so terrified of becoming evil, that I solved the problem by simply..." Joe's voice trailed off.

"By simply what?"

Joe shook his head, unable to respond.

"May I make a presumption that may clarify your confusion?"

Joe looked Money in the eyes, waiting for him to go on.

"You've adopted a view of the world that filters everything through the lens of victims and perpetrators. If you want to leave victimhood, there is only one place to go."

"Yeah," Joe interrupted, "becoming a perpetrator. And that's what I most fear."

"Yes. And you see yourself as being so weak, you fear you will all of a sudden—*poof*—start torturing kittens."

Joe snorted at the thought, and Money continued. "What if you had confidence that you could be tested, and survive? There's only one way to build the muscle of resilience, and that's by continually testing yourself. You don't build muscles by sitting in a chair. Muscles need to be stressed and ripped to grow."

Joe gritted his teeth. "But there *is* good and evil in the world. You know the damage that you, Money, have done in the world."

"Ah, I notice a change in the tone of your voice. What part of you is speaking now?"

"What part?"

"Your face is reddening, your breath is getting shallow, and your leg is bouncing up and down. These are the hallmarks of—"

Joe interrupted through his clenched teeth. "Pissed."

"Now, Pissed, please continue."

"Money, how can you possibly defend money when it drives the world to greed, and the resulting pain, suffering, and cruelty so many people experience?"

Money's face softened. "I know there's a lot of suffering in the world. I see it minute by minute. Humans are both deeply flawed and incredibly generous, creative, loving, and productive. So, Joe, what do you want instead? You've identified a human weakness: greed. So, what do you really want now?"

"I want people to be more caring."

"You're in the good company of centuries of spiritual and trans-formational leaders who want more love and caring."

"Money, please stay specific. We're talking about the problems created by money itself."

"Are we really?"

"I knew you would do that."

"Do what?"

"Try to reframe the issue to avoid the damage that a free-market capitalist system does to the individuals who are left behind."

"... Bingo."

Joe looked up at Money with raised eyebrows.

"Yes, this is where two different models of the world create very different experiences."

"Yes: one model is of caring, and the other is of cruelty. Caring or cruelty? A title for my next article!'"

Money took a long, slow breath. "And since the rich are cruel, you care by being poor? Since you can't trust yourself to be both wealthy and good, you do penance by being poor and righteous? How is this framework working for you and the world?"

Joe clenched his jaw.

"Are you willing to look at a different map of the world?" Money asked.

Joe took a deep breath and paused, letting go of Pissed for the moment. He lay back down on the couch and swung his bare feet up. "Oh Lordy, I sense a major reframe coming."

"A significant one. It takes us from a world of victim and perpe-trator to ownership and agency. Every day, I see both victims and perpetrators. At the same time, I invite you to a world of self-owner-ship. In this world, we intentionally create our own experiences. Ready for the major reframe?"

Joe nodded.

"How we look at the world changes the world itself."

"That's not possible," Joe said, turning his face to the back of the couch, attempting to shut Money's words out.

"The information we take in has to be filtered and edited, or we would be overwhelmed. We need to take bits of data and put them in standard buckets to manage the infinite number of potential distinctions. To do this, we manipulate the incoming information to make it fit our preexisting expectations. We hold beliefs and biases formed from our previous experiences that distort our current experiences. Our memories are movies that we direct and morph over time. Thus, the world we see, feel, touch, taste, and hear is, in effect, a world we create."

Joe turned back to Money with a mocking tone. "So, I can safely run across the freeway if I believe I won't get killed?"

"You can choose how you experience that sprint before you get..." Money raised his eyebrows and tilted his head. "...squished."

"So, are you saying that Sharon, from my article, chose to be fired and poor?" Joe's jaw tightened as Pissed's voice returned.

"What I'm saying is, if she sees herself as a victim in a world of perpetrators, that belief is self-fulfilling. Your article creates a world of perpetrators and victims. By creating the world in those terms, you perpetuate the world in those terms."

"I am not *creating* the world in those terms. I am simply *observing* the world in those terms."

"Is it possible—even if it is just remotely possible—to see the world as full of opportunity, abundance, and generosity?"

Joe sat up and pointed a finger at Money. "Sure, but only if you were born into privilege."

"What about the people who lack privilege and still create a life of fulfillment and richness for themselves? Did their beliefs about the world make that possible?"

"You're blaming the victims for their own pain. It's a heartless position."

"What concerns me is the suffering humans experience as a result of their own beliefs and behaviors. For me, it isn't about blame or shame. Let's say that tomorrow, you, Joe, had the power to create a new economic system that was fair and just. Would the nature of men and women change?"

"No, not immediately. But people would change and adapt because everything was fair."

"The system would manage that?" Money paused to let the thought sink in. "That sounds like a religion with a benevolent system instead of a god. This system, then, will create a world that manages the worst part of how we behave as humans? I've lived among humans since they bartered with cattle and cowrie shells became currency. Humans will twist any and all systems you create to suit themselves. Some systems allow the worst humans to gain power. Some systems reward our creativity and production of value."

Joe sighed, exasperated. "How does all this help Sharon's suffering? Not in theory. I mean real-world action that helps her pay her rent today."

"Joe, you can invite her to create a new set of eyes that can see how she created the world she is living in. These new eyes give her the ability to be creative and make a world for herself that not only feels better, but gets her to her goals."

"She didn't create the world she is living in."

"I can make a list of the financial choices she's made that resulted in her current experience. Would you like that?"

"No," Joe responded petulantly.

"Don't get me wrong, Joe: she's making the best choices she has with what she has to work with. There's no blame or shame. As long as you lock people into the category of 'victims,' and they adopt that mindset, they are locking themselves into a struggle where they're always on the losing side."

Joe's eyes rolled up to the ceiling, hoping for a crushing comeback. "Do you at least recognize that different economic systems create different outcomes?"

"They certainly do! Hundreds of millions of people have been slaughtered and have starved to death because of their own governments' attempts to implement new economic systems. Centralized planning produces consistent results that are not pretty. Opening the menu of choices for all citizens, on the other hand, has had very positive outcomes.

"However, you bring up a great point. If economic and political systems allow the people in power to create enormous suffering, can we design an economic system that reduces suffering? The more we understand how humans create suffering, the more effective we can be. Your article assumes that most human suffering is a result of capitalism. So, Joe, how much of human suffering is the result of economic systems in general?"

"Well, certainly, not all human suffering."

"Excellent. Eventually, all humans die. Parents die. Children die. Brothers and sisters die. And in the march to their inevitable death, humans experience much joy and suffering. The causes of personal suffering are vast and cannot be relieved with only economic or political systems."

Joe slowly stood up and looked directly at Money. "I feel lectured right now. I hate it when you tell me what or how to think."

"Thanks for the heads up. We're moving into a sensitive area. This is good to know. In moving to our higher self, one helpful skill is the ability to entertain different thoughts and still move forward. Can you accept your skepticism and continue?"

"I have no idea what that means. It feels weird."

"Can you feel 'weird' and still consider a new possibility?"

"I've felt weird since your first email, and here we are still talking."

"Joe, your attempt to create a utopian state designed to improve the human experience relies on political power. Political power can't improve the human experience. Historically, over and over again, these externally imposed solutions backfire and create increased suffering. So, let's make a clear distinction between personal suffering and economic systems with all their benefits and constraints. Once you do that, you can look at the root causes of human suffering. That will be far more productive, and far more challenging."

Joe dropped back down onto the couch. "You're playing verbal tricks on me. The thought that I'm hurting people with my articles rather than helping the victims is more than I can bear right now. I'm done for the day, Money. I mean it."

Chapter 15 — When Money Felt Good

"**S**o, you want more money, Joe?"

Joe looked up from his checkbook and credit card statement, the cover letter from the manila envelope still stapled to the legal documents. "Such timing! But I'm still pissed off about our last conversation."

"Yes, that can wait. What is most pressing right now?"

"You know?"

"Of course. It has a paper trail of money, court filing fees, and debts owed, all in my real-time consciousness."

"You're tabulating all that for everyone right now?"

"I have full awareness of all transactions, but of course, I let that go during our discussions. Too distracting." Money paused. "Talk to me, Joe. It's about money, and I am the ultimate resource."

"I got burned by a college roommate on a surefire start-up scheme. I put the funds he needed on my credit card, leaving me on the hook and paying interest and sometimes penalties. The credit card company turned over the debt to a collection agency. By law, they can't hassle me, but they have been anyway. So I ignored them. Now they've sued me, and I have to make a court appearance."

"How much, Joe?"

"Twelve thousand, seven hundred and fifty dollars. If I lose in court, which I will, this letter says I will also be liable for attorneys' fees, collection costs, and interest. I have only thirty days before the court date."

Money paused, as if pulling up all related transactions. "Yes, that matches the points where your story overlaps with monetary exchanges. As you know, I have centuries of experience with this sort of thing. I'll check into it and get back to you."

Joe grinned in spite of himself. "Like I said about a month ago, make it easy and just crap out a big pile of money, and we're good." Joe paused and returned Money's direct eye contact. "Okay, just kidding."

"Excellent. Now, back to my original question: do you want more money?"

"Well, I thought I did. But in the three chairs exercise, I realized the more desperately I want money, the less interest money has in me. And as my voice Pissed so charmingly brought to light, even if I had money, I would hate who I was."

"Whether your focus is on not having money or simply wanting it, you'll continue to struggle."

"What's the alternative? It isn't manifesting stuff, is it?" Joe recalled Julie's mom and Julie's own love-hate relationship with the vision boards, which stopped him short.

Money laughed gently. "Let me tell you a dirty secret. As money, I hear people trying to manifest me all over the place." He paused, and his figure became fuzzy for a moment. "At this very moment, 5,678,284 people are trying to manifest me."

"So what do you do?"

"I ignore them."

"Geez, you have a mean streak."

"No, I have a reality streak. Rewarding people for magical thinking creates beliefs and behaviors that harm not only themselves, but others in their community."

"Okay, so I can't want money—and I can't *not* want money. All this leaves me without any options except to teeter on my financial cliff." Joe looked at the court summons as he spoke.

"And the problem with that?" Money stared at Joe, waiting for a response.

"Women. There, I said it. Some research claims that most women aren't attracted to men who make less than they do. That makes my pool of women pretty dang small."

"Oh, yes. Your credit card statement—the one in your mom's name—has *date me* written all over it."

"Are you here to hurl insults, or is there a higher purpose for this visit?"

"Staying stuck where you are isn't helpful, so let's create clarity for your future. Do you enjoy your work as a journalist?"

"I like writing, but working with publishers can be frustrating... not to mention the fact that I'm just scraping by."

"Do you recall a time, maybe when you were younger, when you worked for someone who was delighted to pay you?"

Joe paused, searching for a memory. "When I was thirteen years old, I used to work for Mrs. McMillan. She was older, and her husband had passed away. I would take out the trash, mow the lawn, wash her car. Household stuff, you know? I remember how she would beam whenever she handed me a ten-dollar bill and told me how happy she was with the work I'd done."

"Excellent example. Mrs. McMillan valued what you did for her—and I suspect your relationship was about more than just the tasks."

"Gosh... it didn't occur to me back then, but yes, I think she was lonely. She would always give me milk and cookies on the days she paid me. And not the store-bought kind. These were made from scratch."

"I think we can safely say that this was a mutually satisfying transaction. Would you agree?"

"Yes, that seems clear."

"Were you motivated only by your need for money?"

"I loved the comic books I was able to buy, but..." Joe paused as his eyes became moist, and his voice softened. "Geez. I haven't thought about her for years. I forgot how nice she was to me."

"If I were human, I would get choked up myself. That was a very tender time for both of you. As Money, I felt honored to be a part of it, and I was very happy to be there."

Joe sighed and wiped his eyes.

"The fact that you're able to bring back your experience with Mrs. McMillan is great news. We can go back to that time in your life and your wonderful relationship with money next time."

"Don't go! I need to talk about the article."

"I'll be back, Joe. Please allow yourself to stay with the feeling you had with Mrs. McMillan. It'll be interesting to see how your world changes while in that state of mind... and maybe even your article."

Chapter 16 — Conflict at the Concert

The day got off to a slow start. Not only had Joe hit the snooze button a few more times than usual, but his computer froze up twice and needed rebooting both times. As much as Joe looked forward to meeting Julie for a concert in the park that afternoon, he could already feel Ian's deadline for the new article looming. After pouring his second cup of coffee, Joe pulled up a Pew study he'd found online.

Skipping over most of the text, he looked ahead to the graphs and charts. One chart showed that children born into the lowest economic bracket had more than a sixty-percent chance of doing better than their parents, with six percent of them making it to the highest bracket. Conversely, for those born at the highest bracket, nearly sixty percent of them would end up worse off than their parents. Surprisingly, nine percent of them would fall into the lowest category! It looked like the poor were getting richer, and the rich were getting poorer. But that couldn't be right; everyone knew it was the other way around. Joe continued reading and lost track of time, unsure whether conventional wisdom could be that far off from the truth, or if he had somehow misunderstood the data. He was surprised when he noticed it was a bit past time to leave to meet Julie for the concert.

Julie was waiting next to one of the pillars near the east entrance of the Presidio. She gave him a quick hug, and they proceeded to an expanse of grass overlooking the Bay. Finding an open space at the foot of the stage, they spread out Julie's blanket. "You fed me last time at dinner, so it's my turn," she said, pulling deli sandwiches and sodas out of her cross-body bag. The orchestra's free public performance was still an hour off, giving them plenty of time to eat and talk. Joe started by giving her a summary of the research he'd found.

"It sounds like it changes 'the poor' from a fixed class into a dynamic..." Julie's voice trailed off as she searched for the right word.

"A dynamic what?"

"I don't know the word for it, but it's kind of like a river that flows with varying volume and eddies, not like a solid riverbed that can be defined once and for all."

"... Are you channeling Heraclitus?"

"Oh, right—you were a philosophy major, so you remember your Greeks."

"Well, I'm not as clear on the topic as I used to be, and some of my conversations with Money have created even more confusion." As he said it, Joe realized he felt safe with Julie and wasn't monitoring his words.

" 'Conversations with money'?" Julie blinked, not following.

Just then, the orchestra filed onto the stage and began tuning up, making further conversation difficult and saving Joe the need to respond. The program started soon after with Debussy's *Spring*, Vivaldi's work of the same name, and Stravinsky's *Rite of Spring*.

After the concert, they picked up their blanket and slowly walked over to a tree near the lake, enjoying an unusually balmy afternoon. Julie restarted the conversation, asking, "So, do you want to tell me more about your new article, and your conversations with money?"

Joe wasn't sure if he was crazy or sane, and surely Julie would think him psycho if he explained his experience. "Money is someone I met in an online forum. He's just a guy who uses 'Money' as a screen name. He's—" Joe stopped suddenly, laughing.

"What's funny?"

"I was about to say he's a lot like you! He doesn't let anything slide." Joe wanted to tell Julie more about his conversations with Money, but he didn't want to appear crazy. Eager to move on, he returned to familiar ground. "In my research for the article, the concept of income mobility is everywhere."

"Is that what it sounds like?"

"Yes: people moving between different economic classes over time. The studies examine different periods of time. Some look at generations, while others use shorter lengths of time, like ten years. But regardless of what's true statistically, I see so many people stuck. I mean, *really* stuck." Joe noticed his voice was tight.

"You don't have any strong feelings about that, do you?" Julie cajoled.

Joe felt a surge of anger, and he recognized the arrival of Pissed. "It's not about me. I see folks in BMWs and Teslas eating pricey food at good restaurants, and I ask myself, 'How many people did they screw to get there?' " Embarrassed by Pissed's appearance, Joe started to withdraw and wall off his feelings.

Julie kept her eyes on him. "Joe, you okay? It seems like you went away for a minute there."

"What you said... I admit it hit home. I've written about the perpetrators for so long, I guess, that..."

Julie quickly finished his sentence. "The thought of making good money, saving for the future, creating a more comfortable life, and perhaps even buying a home and investing for retirement makes you one of *them*?"

Joe's face turned ashen. Her words hit him like a heat-seeking missile.

"Joe, I'm sorry, but your beliefs undermine what I'm building for myself. Look at my boss, Mai. She worked hard, saved money, and opened a business. She's been investing the profits back into the deli, expanding the hours, and introducing new products. I love working for Mai, because I'm learning what it takes to run a business in the black—and I'm getting paid to do it, too."

"She's paying you, but is it a living wage?"

"Oh, I don't know if you'd call it 'living.' " Julie laughed. "I have bigger ambitions, but Mai is paying what she can in money, and much more in skill-building. If she paid more, her prices would go up, and her revenue would go down as her customers switched to her competitors or found other alternatives, like making coffee at home. At that point, the employees also lose, because they're out of a job. That's basic economics."

"Voodoo economics for those duped by the system..." Joe took a deep breath and calmed himself before he spoke again. "I just want things to be better for everyone."

Julie turned to look at the lake as she spoke. "Me too. I also want to have a successful business—and successful businesses have to be reality-based."

"The way vision boards are reality-based?" Joe's voice had more ice in it than he intended.

Julie started to pack her things up in her backpack. "I think it's time to go."

Joe watched her stand up and stride away. Then he just sat there, not moving for a half hour, unable to control the thoughts racing through his mind. Why had he said that? It was almost like Pissed was sabotaging the most wonderful possible relationship he had ever experienced.

Chapter 17 — Walking, Awake, and Anguish

Joe tossed and turned until a needed trip to the bathroom coaxed him out of bed. Having had enough restlessness for one night, he booted up his computer and bounced around obsessively between clickbait and doom-scrolling on social media. The sun rose, casting light around the edges of the blinds, yet it seemed there was a physical weight preventing him from doing any real work. He spent hours in front of the screen, but couldn't remember any single specific thing he'd read.

Later that day, after a mediocre fast-food dinner, he went for a nighttime walk through the Marina Green. As he approached the Palace of Fine Arts, he heard footsteps closing in behind him, provoking an instant surge of adrenaline. He had grabbed his phone in case he needed to dial 911 when a familiar voice called out.

"Joe! We haven't talked for a while; something on your mind?"

"Money! What are you doing out here so late?"

"I don't exactly keep local office hours. And I could ask the same of you, although I have an idea of why you're here."

"Nothing makes sense now. Nothing seems firm."

"What do you want to talk about first—the woman you're dating, economics, or the court date?"

Joe didn't answer immediately, but walked over to a bench with a view of the tan Palace building across the small lake. Money watched him for a minute, then joined him in silence.

"I've made a mistake I can't fix," Joe said at last.

Money raised his eyebrows and tilted his head. "... Oh, with Julie. Let's start with what you're feeling right now."

Joe gave Money a silent assent with a deep breath.

"Now, as you think about your mistake, what comes to mind?"

"I just flashed back to a time in Ms. Halleck's class in third grade. I'd just finished working on a math problem on the blackboard. Ms. Halleck was criticizing me for doing it wrong. My face felt hot, and I almost peed myself. I wanted to hide under the desk, but I had to stand there while she pointed out my stupid mistake to the class. I lost all interest in math that day, and it never came back."

"Do you have similar feelings now when you realize you've made a mistake?"

"It used to be that when someone said I was wrong, I got angry, attacked them, and made them take it back."

"And now?"

"Now, I avoid risky stuff to avoid making mistakes. When I do make a mistake, I just want to cover it up. But it still feels humiliating. It doesn't fit my picture of myself as someone who knows what they are talking about."

"Being right makes you feel worthy? So if someone disagrees with you, they must be wrong, and you need to reject them. Would that be a fair statement?"

Joe considered this for a moment, then nodded his agreement.

"Indeed, nothing can be undone. However, what we learn moves us forward. Most people create an experience of pain in the form of embarrassment, shame, anger, or aggression. However, these reactions don't come with the event; we create the experience with how we think about mistakes. The thought can be either positive or negative, depending on the mindset. It's possible to allow yourself to recognize the impact of a mistake and then just say, 'Okay.' You don't need to cover it up, nor approve of it—just recognize the reality of what happened. Once you've acknowledged the situation, you can ask, 'What do I want now?'"

"I know what I *don't* want: I don't want to feel the way I do!"

"And what's the cost of avoiding those feelings?"

"Cost? What cost?"

"When you avoid the feelings, what happens? What does it cost you?"

Joe's lips tightened. "It takes a lot of work to avoid the pain."

"As you say these words aloud, what do you notice?"

"Oh, God, what am I feeling? Sorrow, loss, despair, helplessness... Is awareness supposed to help?"

"You've experienced a significant loss, and you have regrets. The good news is that you can start looking at it and learning from it, and make choices that work better for you. You don't have to repeat old mistakes. Instead, you can move on to new ones."

Joe chuckled. "Make new ones? That's supposed to encourage me?"

"Humor is one of the most powerful tools we have for defusing the negative feelings around mistakes that keep us stuck. When you find the humor in a situation, it takes the sting away and allows the lesson to become clear."

Joe nodded in understanding.

"You're building up emotional muscles. As they get stronger, difficult things get easier. We can practice right now. Are you game?"

"In the middle of the night on a bench in the park?"

Money just tilted his head and raised his eyebrows.

"I guess I have nothing else scheduled for the next few minutes. So, what's the game?"

"In this game, you are the creator of a movie. You script, direct, act in, and produce a movie called *Joe's Many Mistakes*. Start with the earliest 'mistakes' you can remember. Then, play out the scene in your mind with as much detail as you can—only this time, from the mindset that you're okay, curious, and eager to learn from each event."

"You mean like when you're watching a movie, and you know the good guy is doing something dumb?"

"Or more like, 'What can I learn?' What perspective or beliefs does the hero have that limit what they see or know? So, play all the scenes that you've replayed in your head dozens or hundreds of times. To do this, close your eyes for focus, and start with the earliest painful memories."

Joe closed his eyes and was surprised at how quickly the parts of his movie came back to him. He had written the scripts long ago and acted them out over and over in his mind. The theme that they all had in common was a justification for his anger. He sat quietly on the bench, exploring his feelings around his past experiences, including disappointments, losses, and mistakes. He noticed that although he still felt tender while reliving these moments, Money was right: the tug of these events didn't feel as strong when he watched them with curiosity.

As he stepped into each experience, he noticed he was aware of observing the discomfort while feeling it at the same time. But it was more like watching a movie rather than *being* the movie. He thought about Ms. Halleck, and felt a rush of sympathy for young Joe. A mental movie of the scene where his angry father spanked him came back quickly, as did the scene of a classmate laughing at him when he asked her to the school dance.

"What are you noticing that you didn't see before?" Money's voice had a hypnotic tone, allowing Joe to both reexperience each previous memory and be curious about what he could learn.

After about fifteen minutes, Joe opened his eyes.

"Joe, welcome back. Please take three slow, deep breaths."

Joe felt as though a weight had been lifted off of him. For the first time in days, he felt tired, but an *honest* tired.

He turned to thank Money, but there was no one there. Then his phone pinged with a text message. It was from Money.

Call your friend about the money you lent him on your credit card ASAP.

Joe walked back to his apartment and climbed into bed.

Morning came quickly, and he woke up with new ideas for articles and a new text from Money: *Call him now.* But Joe's focus on the text was quickly replaced by the thought of his mistake with Julie. For a moment, he'd forgotten their fight and how he reacted. He felt himself start the slippery slide into the comfort zone of his old context of victimhood and resentment. But this time, something different happened—something very different. At that exact moment, he knew he didn't want to fall into his old beliefs. Instead, he decided to play the movie game again. The practical framework that Money had given him was immediately helpful. Joe rewatched their conversation in the park, with three questions at the top of his mind: what had he missed, how did he react, and how could he learn from the experience?

Chapter 18 — Certificates of Appreciation

"**I** have something for you, Joe."

Joe struggled out of a deep sleep. It was 6:00 a.m., and the glowing digits on his clock whispered, 'Sleep... sleep, my love.'

Money, however, had other ideas. "Look at your nightstand," he said.

Joe reached for the lamp and knocked it over. Swearing, he straightened the lamp, hit the switch, and immediately was shocked into full awareness. A pile of hundred-dollar bills sat within arm's reach.

"Is this for me?" Joe asked, amazed. "Or is this another exercise?"

"It is both for you *and* an exercise."

"One hundred plus reasons not to be upset about the early-morning start," Joe said. "Okay, I'll bite. What's the exercise?"

"Remember the first Golden Key?"

"Awareness."

"That's right. And what are you aware of right now?"

"I have to pee."

Caught by surprise, Money roared with laughter. "Okay. How about I meet you in the kitchen?"

Joe shuffled in a short while later and quickly heated up a cup of stale coffee in the microwave.

Sitting at the small bistro table, Money put the hundred-dollar bills in front of Joe, who slowly counted to ten with reverence. "What are you aware of right now?"

"The smell of new money competing with old coffee. That's a first."

"What else?"

"My breathing is shallow, and my heart is racing a bit."

"Now, move your awareness down through your body."

Joe took another breath. "I have butterflies in my stomach. My thighs are tight, and my left leg is bouncing up and down." Joe reached out and fingered the crisp, new cash.

"Now, let's concentrate for a moment on what you're feeling. Do you notice any emotional shifts as you pick up the bills?"

"Normally, I feel... I don't know, just blah or gray, or even nothing at all. But right now, I'm excited."

"Does this excitement feel good?"

"It shouldn't, but it does."

"Now, take a moment and focus on the thoughts that are coming and going through your head. When you're aware of a thought or string of thoughts, say them out loud. This is where SET practice pays off."

"How can I notice my thoughts as they happen? I mean, if you *think* about your thoughts, then that thinking becomes your thoughts, no?"

"With practice, you can become an observer of your thoughts. Just take a moment and, without judgment, notice what you're thinking."

Joe's eyes rolled upwards for a moment, as if searching for an elusive something. "I'm having lots of thoughts, and they're coming rapid fire. I'm thinking about what I could do with this money.

I could take Julie out to a nice dinner and apologize. Oh, wow—now I have a critical voice telling me I am going to make a mistake."

"How is the experience of this money you're holding different from the experience of receiving money from Mrs. McMillan?"

"I get a rush of excitement thinking of all the things this money could do for me, but it's not like the satisfaction I got when Mrs. McMillan handed me her limited money."

Money looked at the hundred-dollar bill Joe was still holding. "Okay. So that piece of paper in your hand—what does it represent?"

"No matter what I say, it's going to be wrong, and you're going to 'reframe' it."

"We're not trying to find the truth here, Joe, just trying to increase your awareness, so that you can accept yourself fully and completely as you are." Money paused and grinned. "And you're right. I probably do have a reframe for you."

Joe snorted and shook his head, but responded, "These pieces of paper are representations of money. And I know what you are going to ask: what does money represent? Right?"

"Yes."

"Money represents payments you've received. Somebody pays your salary, or somebody buys something from you, and they give you money."

"So, do people give you that money voluntarily, or under duress?"

"Unless I point a gun at them, I guess they give it to me voluntarily."

"So, why would they voluntarily give you money?"

"Because they want what I have more than they want the hundred-dollar bill."

"And you give them what they want in exchange for that hundred-dollar bill voluntarily?"

"I've never been forced to take a hundred-dollar bill and then been expected to give them something in return. Maybe that's because I never met the Godfather."

"I have... And no, you don't want to be on the other side of the Godfather's offers. Now, back to that transaction. It's voluntary on both sides. Agreed?"

"Yes."

"Can we then assume that both sides, at that moment, perceive the value they receive in that transaction to be beneficial?"

Joe nodded. "Both of us received more value than we gave up. And we did so voluntarily."

"Good summary. I gave you those hundred-dollar bills in appreciation for our time together—a down payment for the book you'll write."

Joe smiled and shook his head. "I find both the conversation *and* the money valuable. So, I guess I can't lose."

Money laughed. "From that mutually satisfying experience, I transcend being just money and become a *Certificate of Appreciation*."

Joe giggled nervously and shifted uncomfortably in his chair as Money continued.

"What stops you from embracing money as Certificates of Appreciation?"

Joe snorted. "Just thinking that thought makes me nervous."

"Okay, let's take a different tack. What if there was someone similar to you, but not you, who believed and acted totally and completely *as if* money were a Certificate of Appreciation? What would their life be like if they held that belief and acted on it?"

"It's hard to even conceive of."

"Humor me here. Allow yourself to stay with the experience of discomfort for a moment. What if someone similar to you, but not you, totally and thoroughly believed that money was a Certificate of Appreciation, with no negative baggage?"

Several emotions rippled across Joe's face as he considered all the ramifications. "If someone similar to me felt that money was simply a Certificate of Appreciation, and that guy was a good guy..." Suddenly, Joe stopped speaking, and he felt his stomach tighten.

"Now, to be able to continue that thought, it will help to take several deep breaths."

Joe nodded and focused on each breath until he reached a rhythm that was slow and deep.

"Good work, Joe. What are your physical sensations right now?"

"I think I'm going to be okay."

" 'Think'?" Money paused with a grin.

Joe laughed as he felt the relief of letting go of his survival reactions.

"Now that you know you're going to survive this," Money said, "tell me what might happen with a person like you, who lived a life where money represented Certificates of Appreciation."

"He would be free. He would be free of the burden and weight that I feel on my shoulders."

Money nodded in solemn agreement.

Two days later, the *ping* of an incoming email interrupted Joe's focus. With the Themis deadline looming large, he'd managed to push all talk of Certificates of Appreciation out of his head. Now the concept came rushing back into his brain as soon as he read the subject line.

From: Money <money@conversations.money>
To: Joe Everie <JoeEverie@gmail.com>
Subject: Getting comfortable with those Certificates

Dear Joe,

I know you want some time to allow the idea of Certificates of Appreciation to settle in. One way to make the concept real is an exercise that give you practice making the CoA's real. Any confusion will clear up as soon as you make this practice a habit.

I put this exercise in your online account.

—Money

P.S. Call your deadbeat friend NOW.

They'd ended their last conversation with Joe's realization that if money were truly a Certificate of Appreciation, he could collect it without guilt, conflict, or burden. He knew he'd have to revisit this reframe before it truly took hold. Despite the unfortunate timing of the email, Joe knew Money was doing his best to give him the tools to do so. After doing an SET check, Joe quickly banged out a reply.

From: Money <money@conversations.money>
To: Joe Everie <JoeEverie@gmail.com>
Subject: Under the gun

Thanks, Money, but I'm feeling the pinch when it comes to getting that new Themis article out the door. I will listen to this later. Right now, getting a few Certificates of Appreciation in my account is a top priority. (How do you like that? I'm in such a rush, I don't even have time to cringe at the phrase!)

—Joe

P.S. OK...ok, will call him.

Certificates of Appreciation — Making it Real

Issue: We make financial transactions out of habit and don't fully appreciate how many people are involved in delivering that value to us.

Exercise Description: This exercise creates a new mental model of money as a Certificate of Appreciation in your everyday transactions. Every time you have a financial transaction, you will create a verbal anchor that expresses it in terms of Certificates of Appreciation.

Outcome: By expanding your appreciation of your financial transactions, you will also appreciate the value you deliver to others. This process will create a new habit that reduces stress and increases joy.

Time to Complete: A few seconds, for a lifetime

Prerequisites: Read the chapter "Certificates of Appreciation."

Exercise Access: You will find detailed instructions in your complimentary online course.

Join or log into your complimentary online course here:
https://conversations.money/book-exercises/

Chapter 19 — Money, Value, and Force

J oe's finger shook as he hit the red button that ended the call. He looked up from his phone. "You there? Money? Hello... ?"

Joe blinked, surprised to find himself alone. "Great. Now I'm talking to myself." He returned to his work and continued typing.

Thirty seconds later, Money's voice boomed as the voice of Lurch, a servant from a sixties TV sitcom. "You rang?"

Joe missed the humor. He turned, happy to find Money standing in the kitchen doorway. "I thought I heard you just now! But truth be told, I'm happy you're here. I called him."

"Him?"

"Yes, *him*. He is going to pay me back."

"Really?" Money responded in mock surprise.

"You knew!"

"I know all things money."

"You mean you knew that my deadbeat friend managed to sell the patent from his failed company? He said he got an email from a stranger who put him onto a large company using his patent. He said he had no idea how much it was worth. I don't think he would have paid me if I hadn't called. Thanks, I owe you. I really mean it; I owe you so much. I'm so relieved, like shaky relief. As soon as the wire transfer hits my account, I can pay the credit card debt, and the court date disappears."

Money crossed the room, leaned in, and said softly, "Do you remember the first time we met?"

"Yes. Back then, I suspected I was going crazy. But if this is crazy, it's working."

"How do you feel right now?"

"Hopeful. Really hopeful! I feel like a concrete block has been lifted from my shoulders. Now I can start looking forward to the future with more confidence."

"Excellent. So, what does the future hold for Joe Everie?"

"Slow down. Right now, my future is in about one hour. I'm working out a few issues for this article, but something still doesn't make sense." Joe got up and stood in front of the grimy window overlooking the street. "When I step into your shoes and look at you as a representation of value delivered, it makes sense for a brief moment. But when I look at the world through my own eyes and see all the cruelty and suffering, I feel anger again. There must be something to represent value other than money. Money drives people to war. Money makes divorces ugly. Businesses cheat customers to get more money. People who don't have enough money steal to survive."

"I'll be the first to acknowledge the tremendous amount of suffering in the world. If you look at all suffering, what percentage do you think actually comes from money? What's your guess? Think about broken hearts, physical abuse, racism, murder, sexism, loneliness, rape, sickness, death, depression, and betrayal."

"I guess Money isn't central to that kind of pain."

"So, of all the pain and suffering, what part do I play?"

"Can that even be measured?"

"Here's what I've observed. There's one metric that's a major contributor to the amount of financial suffering many people experience: *financial suffering intensifies when people separate money from value.* The larger the gap, the greater the suffering. The struggle you're experiencing is perpetuated by seeking money, for yourself or others, without creating and delivering value."

"That sounds too absolute to be true."

"Of course! But this simplified concept can be useful. As you look at the world, look for gaps where money is separated from delivering value. Just be curious and notice."

"I see the connection, but even if I were to see money only as a representation of value, the rest of the world uses it very differently! I live in a world where money is used to abuse people." Joe's voice became noticeably tight with the unexpected emotional response.

"Joe, you couldn't have said it better. That's why I invite you to write a book about money and value."

"Do you expect me to write a book that will convince evil people to adopt a value-based monetary system?"

"That would be wonderful... but let's leave it for the second book."

Joe laughed despite himself. "First, it was a conversation. Then it was writing a book. Now you want a sequel? Where is this going to end—a stage play?"

"I prefer a musical, but your call."

Joe laughed again.

"My immediate concern is not the evil people in the world right now," Money went on, "but the good-hearted people of the world who have disassociated money from value. My biggest fear is that the good people of this world will reject the value of money, demonize wealth, and in the ensuing vacuum, it will be replaced with brute force."

"Money and brute force? I don't get the connection."

"Let's start at the beginning and work slowly."

"Yeah, yeah, I know the drill. Sometimes it is helpful, but other time it feels condescending."

"Which is it this time?"

"Condescending, I think. It's like you have the truth, and you're patiently helping me discover it."

Money remained silent, allowing Joe the time to answer his own question.

"But if I reframe it and focus on your positive intention of clarifying our conversation, well, I guess this feels fine. So, build away."

"Do you realize what you just did? You made a critical distinction between the event and the meaning. You took charge and became the agent of the meaning, rather than letting the event come prepackaged with emotional triggers. With that reframe, you are in charge of your experience and are able to look at a different model of the world with curiosity. With the confidence that you can explore new models without feeling threatened, we can indeed start building a thought experiment."

Joe blushed, slightly embarrassed by the high praise.

"I do have a model that fits centuries of experience," Money continued. "It's a way of looking at the world that will serve humans better when adopted. You're always at choice, which means you can accept or reject my invitation to step into a new way of thinking.

" 'At choice.' That's an awkward phrase."

"Yes, intentionally. It stands out to create a fresh reframe to encourage agency, your ability to determine meaning of events. Then, after doing so, you can decide which parts work for you, and which don't. Can you play with a new model, just for now?"

After thinking about this for a moment, Joe nodded. "Why not?"

"Great! So, is your life of value to you?"

"Do we have to go that far back? I mean, we know my life is valuable to me."

"Yes, and one step at a time. So, your life is valuable, and I assume that you want to stay alive as long as possible?"

"Yeah, even as shitty as it is. In the past..." Joe trailed off, not quite sure how to continue, or even if he needed to.

"It's okay," Money said. "Just stay open to the experience."

"Alright."

"Your life is valuable to you. So, how do you keep yourself alive? For example, air to breathe, water to drink, and food to eat—how do you get those things?"

"The air is free, as long as I'm not in a windowless box. Water, food, and shelter, I buy with money."

"So, other than air, everything else requires cooperation with others in your community?"

"Well, I don't personally know the people who create all that stuff that makes my life better!"

"Good point. I was thinking of everyone connected to you in a community of suppliers. However we use the word, it still sounds like you're in collaboration and cooperation for the very needs that keep you alive. True?"

"True."

"So, let's look at the opposite: If you weren't in voluntary collaboration with these people, how would you get them to supply your eggs for breakfast? An involuntary collaboration? In other words, the use of force?"

"I see where you're going. How about I whiz through these steps and save us both some time? First, I can't live in isolation. I need stuff from others, but I can't use force because I don't have that power—or if I used it, I'd be arrested. So that means I need to create voluntary relationships. And the most efficient way of doing that is by using—ta-da..." Joe paused for emphasis and waved an imaginary wand. "... MONEY!"

"But what if you did have a lot of power?"

"I wouldn't need money, because I could force people and torture them if they didn't give me what I wanted." Joe grinned at this thought that was so unlike him.

Money started to comment, then closed his mouth for a few moments. "Did I lose you in your fantasies of power?"

"Just joking."

"Really?" Money paused. "So, if we don't want to go down that road, then we're left without the use of force. Is this distinction clear? We can engage with others using degrees of power, force, and manipulation, or we can engage in voluntary relationships. Now, here is the punch line. *If a lot of good people eschew money because it's associated with evil rich people, we leave a vacuum that diminishes voluntary cooperation.* That vacuum is a magnet for people who love power. Money is the *currency* used by people who want to cooperate for mutual benefit. Without that voluntary exchange, evil people introduce the currency of force."

Joe searched for a counterexample while Money waited patiently. Finally, Joe looked away, unable to formulate his thoughts.

"I've been around since man invented me," Money continued. "Every time a culture rejects me as evil, power fills the vacuum. But it always comes dressed up as caring, justice, fairness, righteous revenge, sacrifice, or equality."

"Are you sure?" Joe muttered weakly.

"Russia's Bolshevik revolution decreed a transfer of land to peasants, worker control over production, and distribution of bread to the cities. The czars had indeed cruelly mistreated the peasants—but no fewer than twenty million Soviet citizens died due to Bolshevik's idealism. Do you want more examples, Joe?"

"No. You were there, and you can easily out-history me."

"Good people often end up supporting raw power today in the quest for a better world tomorrow. However, political and economic systems still reflect who we are as humans. As long as human nature remains in its present state, visualizing a utopia without human spiritual or humanistic transformation just leaves us open to political con artists. Utopian ideals, with the best of intent can't change human nature through politics. This is because the government is made up of humans whose only tool is force or threat of force. With the government's inevitable shortcomings and outright failures, those in power feel compelled to use even more force to produce utopia. The end of this movie is the compounded misery of millions of people who just want to live ordinary lives."

"Money, you just fell into your own trap. Isn't this the same process that a capitalist economy goes through: the rich get richer and use the power of money to force others to enrich them even further?"

"As long as the capitalist doesn't have the right to use force or the threat of imprisonment, the damage is limited."

"What you just said—I realize that I ignored something significant."

"Something?"

"Yes: I didn't think about human motivation. I ignored your assertion that human nature is the same under all economic systems. I assumed that somehow the system determined human behavior. I assumed that a changed system would create changed people. So, what we're talking about is understanding 'human nature.' This leads us to the big question: what type of system invites us to embody our higher selves? We have evolved from tribal instincts for the most part. Can we make this evolution more intentional?"

Money remained silent, as if stunned.

"... Money?"

"Yes, Joe?"

"You're quiet."

"In appreciation and honor of your thoughtfulness."

Joe stepped into the kitchen for a glass of water. He returned a minute later, fired up and ready to continue, but Money was gone.

Joe shrugged, knowing the clock was ticking on his article and Money would undoubtedly return.

"Money Speech" — Choose Your Experience

Issue: Our cultural beliefs about money and its role in our economy and political and civil society have shifted without awareness and without conscious choice.

Exercise Description: In this exercise, you will read a famous chapter from a book written in 1957 that puts forth a very stark set of money beliefs. After you read the description, you will take an assessment of your reactions.

Outcome: Make a conscious choice about your money model. Because of the clarity of the position put forth, without apology, you will have the opportunity to bring into conscious awareness your own beliefs and make changes that feel better and honor your deepest values.

Time to Complete: About one hour

Prerequisites: None

Exercise Access: You will find detailed instructions in your complimentary online course.

Join or log into your complimentary online course here:

https://conversations.money/book-exercises/

Chapter 20 — Riches and Resentment

The sun was directly overhead, filling every corner of the small concrete park with light. A homeless couple wrapped in stained sleeping bags slept on the curving walkway, while a knot of young men played a game of cards near the park's entrance. Joe and Money strolled over to a pair of benches near the swing set, each sitting on his own bench. Joe glanced around, not surprised that no children were in sight.

Money wasted no time launching into the real meat of the day's conversation. "So, tell me about people who have lots of money."

"Like, money to burn?" Joe stifled a grin.

"Thinking of me on fire is amusing?"

Joe laughed, happy to be sharing this beautiful summer day with Money. *He was surprised to find himself enjoying the companionship, and even admitting the pleasure to himself. Then he remembered Julie, the only other person who...*

"Hello, Joe... ? Money to Joe. You want to immolate me?"

"Of course not. It's a line from a song that popped into my head."

"Onward, then. I asked you to tell me about people who have lots of money. Can you think of a specific rich person who fits the bill? Imagine this person in vivid detail. Is it a man or a woman?"

"A man."

"Describe him."

Joe laughed. "Pissed just popped into my head and vigorously objects."

"Great. He'll give us some clues about hidden anchors to wealth."

Joe took a moment to allow Pissed to find his voice. "Well, this rich guy made his money screwing everybody over. He didn't pay his employees well. He cheated on his taxes—hell, maybe even cheated on his wife—but now this asshole is rich because he made a killing selling shoddy product that no one needed, but everyone kept buying them anyway! Joe plays by the rules—yet this total jackass just plays golf every day!"

"Thank you, Pissed, for being so clear! And what rules does Joe play by?"

"Be nice. Work hard. Keep your head down. And don't complain."

"Who made these rules?"

"Our culture."

"Does everyone in your culture obey these rules?"

"Of course not! Only the nice guys."

"And then the nice guys get screwed?"

"Yes! You finally get it!" Joe raised his arms in emphasis.

"So you obey a set of rules where you're the chump?"

Joe started to react, but instead, he came back to his own voice. "I don't know how to answer that."

Money hesitated for a moment. "Pissed is good at being pissed. Complex issues are lost on him. It could very well be that you have unexamined rules for your life that no longer serve you. As you bring them to the surface and shine a light on them, their lack of clarity becomes more evident. Fortunately, I have an assessment that may help with this."

"You have an assessment?"

"To be included in your book." Money pulled a piece of paper from his jacket pocket and handed it to Joe. "Do you need a pen?"

Joe shook his head and pulled a pen from his messenger bag. "I'm a writer, remember?"

Joe spent the next half hour carefully filling out the checkboxes and adding his thoughts to the comments section. He handed it back to Money and asked for another copy. Money looked at him curiously.

"Don't ask," Joe said.

Joe filled out the second copy faster and with intensity. He thrust it back into Money's hands. Money held the forms side by side.

"When I filled out the first one, I wanted to answer using the voice of a victim in the system. I realized this was coming from Pissed, so I did it twice."

Money nodded in approval. "I appreciate your ability to be aware of Pissed and your new ways of thinking at the same time. Acceptance is the key to unlocking the underlying positive intention he has for you."

"The second Golden Key, right?"

"Exactly. Now, let's look at the two responses."

Joe abandoned his bench and sat beside Money.

Exercise: Hidden Anchors to Wealth

Hidden Anchors to Wealth

Issue: Our emotional reactions are associated with words and language and are often automatic and outside our conscious awareness. Language can trigger past associations that are not helpful to your values or goals.

Exercise Description: This exercise will give you a list of terms. As you read the words, notice your immediate visceral reaction. Your score will be tallied, and the results will be emailed to you.

Outcome: Bring into awareness your linguistic emotional triggers, giving you the opportunity to reframe them to align with your actual core values.

Time to Complete: 15 minutes

Prerequisites: None

Exercise Access: You will find detailed instructions in your complimentary online course.

Join or log into your complimentary online course here:
https://conversations.money/book-exercises/

Please complete this exercise before reading Joe's results.

Riches and Resentment – Money Reviews Pissed's Responses

	Very Positive	Mildly Positive	Mildly Negative	Very Negative	Comments
Wealthy people				✓	Stuck up and arrogant and don't deserve what they have
Private jets			✓		Environmentally harmful and unnecessary
Large corporations				✓	Heartless and only concerned about money
Stock market			✓		Where wealthy people screw everyone else
Investing		✓			Only for the rich, the poor can't participate
Capitalism			✓		Rules made for the rich to get richer
Free markets				✓	Unregulated greed
Windfall profits				✓	Undeserving
Money			✓		Root of evil
Private property			✓		Protecting the rich
Profits				✓	Made by squeezing workers
Sales strategies			✓		Manipulation for mindless consumerism
Advertising			✓		Same as manipulation
CEO bonus			✓		Reward for greed
Bankers				✓	Managing the money of the rich to get richer
Mansions				✓	Waste of the environment
Extravagance				✓	Show they are better than you
Savings accounts		✓			So hard to build with rules that favor the rich
Rolls Royce				✓	Conspicuous consumption
Rolex				✓	Conspicuous consumption
Deregulation			✓		Remove the constraints for greedy people
Inheritance			✓		The privileged inherit the spoils of war
Private schools			✓		Give the advantages of education and connection to the elite
Wall Street			✓		Ground zero for what is wrong with America
Plant closing			✓		Screw the workers for more profits
Tax avoidance				✓	Yes, let the poor pay
Lower taxes for all		✓			How about no taxes for the rest of us?
Libertarians			✓		Screwballs that lead to anarchy
Conservatives			✓		Pushing their morals on us
Billionaires			✓		Using their money to stomp on us
Bosses			✓		Drive by profits, not people
The 1%			✓		They don't know what our lives are like

Money quickly tallied the score on the first assessment with just a glance. "If I add up Pissed's score and give each response a +3 for

'Very Positive,' a +1 for 'Mildly Positive', and balance that with a -1 for 'Mildly Negative' and a -3 for 'Very Negative,' Pissed gets a score of -45."

"Wow. Pissed is aptly named, if I do say so myself. When I step into his voice, it all feels so real."

"We can discuss that in a moment. Now, let's add up Joe's score. Is it okay to call it Joe's score?"

"Uh..."

"Humor me for a moment."

"Sure."

"This one has very different responses."

	Very Positive	Mildly Positive	Mildly Negative	Very Negative	Comments
Wealthy people		✓			If they deliver value
Private jets			✓		Wasteful
Large corporations		✓			If they help people work together to deliver value
Stock market		✓			Investors can particpate in the profits of delivering value
Investing		✓			A goal for everyone.
Capitalism		✓			Works great if money is a Certificate of Appreciation
Free markets		✓			Only if we are free to add value to others
Windfall profits		✓			Maybe someone anticipated future needs?
Money	✓				Really a Certificate of Appreciation
Private property		✓			You own yourself and what you produce
Profits		✓			If they are made by contributing real value
Sales strategies		✓			Are they designed to meet real needs?
Advertising			✓		Can be manipulative or communicating something of value
CEO bonus			✓		If rewarded for delivering value, not how many receive bonuses even after making major mistakes
Bankers				✓	So many scandals and screwing customers rather than delivering value.
Mansions			✓		Waste of the environment
Extravagance			✓		They need things to show they are worthwhile or better than us.
Savings accounts		✓			A collection of Certificates of Appreciation. Collect more!
Rolls Royce				✓	Conspicuous consumption
Rolex				✓	Conspicuous consumption
Deregulation		✓			Do regulations limit the delivery of value? Can we eliminate just those?
Inheritance			✓		People who didn't create value receive the benefits of those who did. Not sure this is right
Private schools		✓			Can we find a way to deliver great education like this to everyone?
Wall Street		✓			Helping move capital to those who can deliver the most value?
Plant closing			✓		Maybe they weren't delivering value?
Tax avoidance			✓		The wealthy pay the most taxes. Eliminate loopholes.
Lower taxes for all		✓			How about no taxes for most of us?
Libertarians		✓			Do they want rules to take advantage or create more options to engage others voluntarily?
Conservatives			✓		Pushing their morals on us
Billionaires		✓			Boy, some of them delivered a lot of value!
Bosses		✓			Creating jobs, work, cooperation to deliver value
The 1%			✓		Even if they earned their money, they become arrogant and elite.

"I was thinking of you and Julie when I filled it out," Joe said. "But, to be clear, I added qualifiers in the comments."

"Noted. Using the same scoring rules, you have a total of +2, compared to Pissed's -45. Right now, Joe, you are aware of both universes and contexts."

"Yeah, and I can step in and out of either of them. It used to be I had just one truth. It told me everything I needed to know about the world and what to think. It goes back to that bad experience at camp, where I had one foot in the canoe and one foot on the dock."

"Ready for a magic word?"

" 'Reframe'?'"

"Yes, 'reframe'! Before we started our conversations, you had certainty. You filtered everything you saw, heard, read, and studied through that belief system. You needed to defend yourself because that truth was part of who you were and gave you importance. Now look at you! You can step into one world, experience that world, respond from that world, and then intentionally step into a different world."

"It still feels like I'm gonna fall in the lake."

"Or maybe this time, you can gracefully move back and forth between the canoe and the dock."

Chapter 21 — The Extravagant Money Model

J oe glanced up at Money, then went back to the task at hand, not at all surprised by the sudden appearance of his mentor. It wasn't that Joe felt an urgent need to blow on the steaming bowl of ramen noodles in front of him; he was simply so comfortable with Money that he no longer felt compelled to make a big deal out of his arrival.

After watching Joe for a few moments, Money said, "It only takes sixty seconds to nuke that stuff, you know?"

"Not in this piece-of-crap microwave. No matter how I set it, this ramen—"

"—Bowl of sodium—"

"—*Delicious* bowl of sodium is either too hot or too cold."

"Is there anything on your mind more pressing than these lunchtime struggles? Because I distinctly felt your call."

Joe responded in a British accent. "Why, yes, Money. There is!" With a touch of over-the-top flair, he twirled some noodles around his fork. Then he dug in, talking between bites. "I concede that Certificates of Appreciation are a way to measure the value that's delivered. But once so many Certificates are collected, it changes the character of most people. They lose empathy and the ability to feel what it's like to live a hand-to-mouth existence. And eventually, day after day, their caring disappears—that is, if they ever had it at all."

"Great observation. Yes, wealth and power are an aphrodisiac to human brain chemistry—an aphrodisiac that's especially alluring to people who haven't expanded their humanity. For some, wealth and power are an attempt to fill a chronic hole in their heart."

"Like an addiction?"

"Yes, like an addiction."

"If that's the case, we can equalize a money addiction by taxing the rich. Less money, less temptation."

"Yes, we've discussed that. What would be the experience of those who had the power to use force or threat of force to take someone else's Certificates of Appreciation? Remember our discussion about power and force? Power has even a greater addictive impact on the brain than wealth."

"And you know this because..."

"Centuries of empirical observation. Your book will encourage your readers to think and think deeply about the corruption of power. It can also create another powerful distinction."

"Distinction between what?"

"If you use power to gain money, can that really be a Certificate of Appreciation?"

"How about we just call it 'filthy lucre' and be done with it?"

"The phrase I like is 'Bills of Indictment.' It's a distinction that requires some depth of thought, but it has a big payoff. I have centuries of information about the differences between countries that produce significant Bills of Indictment and countries that operate mostly with Certificates of Appreciation. Countries that turn a significant number of Certificates of Appreciation into Bills of Indictment correlate with strong leaders, totalitarianism, and crony capitalism. The wealth gap between the politically favored and the poor is huge. In these countries, most of the wealth is represented by Bills of Indictment—or in other words, loot. All countries have Bills of Indictment to some extent. But it might surprise you to know that worldwide, Certificates of Appreciation outnumber Bills of Indictment by many times. Thousands of times, even millions of times. In countries where this isn't the case, they pave the road to ruin."

"So, money can be both an indictment and a token of appreciation?"

Money nodded solemnly.

"I have to tell you, this is getting crazy. I mean, if you extend this thought, then wealthy people who have a lot of Certificates of Appreciation..."

Joe paused mid-sentence with a look of discomfort on his face. Money waited for him to continue.

"... Some people might come to the conclusion that the more money you make, the wealthier you are, the more value you've contributed to the world."

"I'm delighted! You've worked this through and are starting to see the consequences."

"But what about people like Martin Luther King, Jr., Mahatma Gandhi, and Mother Teresa? What about parents who stay home to take care of their kids? Or people like doctors who volunteer to go to the poorest places?"

"Indeed! There are many ways to deliver value to your family, your community, and the broader world. In fact, I'd say that most of the value we provide to others has nothing to do with me. Think of the importance of parental love for a newborn child. Without love and touch and a sense of well-being, the child would wither and die, even if it were born a king."

Joe took a deep breath and blew it out through clenched teeth. "If there are ways to make a bigger impact outside of just making money, doesn't that make working for money more like working for mammon? The Bible says that you cannot serve God and mammon."

"I know you grew up as a Christian, but that was long ago. Now you're quoting Scripture?"

"Alright, you busted me. I'm grasping."

"Excellent admission. But what is mammon to you, Joe?"

"In my mind, it represents greed, wealth, and worshiping money."

"May I quote the full passage from the book of Matthew?"

"You've got it memorized?"

Money smiled. "Chalk it up to ego. Here's Matthew 6:19–21 and 24 in the King James version of the New Testament: 'Lay not up for yourselves treasures upon earth, where moth and rust doth corrupt, and where thieves break through and steal: But lay up for yourselves treasures in heaven, where neither moth nor rust doth corrupt, and where thieves do not break through nor steal: For where your treasure is, there will your heart be also. No man can serve two masters: for either he will hate the one, and love the other; or else he will hold to the one, and despise the other. Ye cannot serve God and mammon.' "

"I smell a biblical reframe coming. Isn't it a wee bit above your pay grade?"

Money laughed. "Joe, I appreciate you more and more with each conversation. If we look at money as an end in and of itself as an object of worship, we can label it 'mammon.' If our heart's only desire is to accumulate money, it's difficult to live a life from our higher self. But what if our goal were not to accumulate money, but to deliver value? Could it be that providing value to God's children is serving God?"

"Tell me you're not promoting prosperity theology. You know those prosperity preachers push the offering plate, right?" Joe grinned, amused at his alliteration.

"Yes; I would even say that some of them are mammon's ultimate disciples. No, Joe, I'm not preaching 'prosperity theology,' where God rewards the faithful with wealth, even though some of the language I use is similar. But for now, I'd like to get back to the concept of Certificates of Appreciation. I'd like to clarify an important distinction. Imagine having a photograph of you with your loving family. Imagine wanting more pictures of you with different loving families. You arrange to get more and more of these taken. You're so desperate that you even photo-edit yourself into pictures of other loving families."

Joe smirked. "That is the dumbest thing I've ever heard. The pleasure is in creating a loving family in the first place, not just being in the picture."

"Yet many people are simply collecting currency, which is nothing more than printed pieces of paper with pictures of dead rulers on them. They act as if they were valuable in and of themselves."

Joe remained silent, feeling the impact of the analogy.

Money's voice softened. "Yes, what a liberating notion when we focus on value instead of money."

For a moment, Joe's internal voices bounced back and forth between his two worlds. Finally, he took a deep breath. "So, what you're saying is that money, when it's... uh... respected... When you respect money as a product of delivering value, that's very different from loving money in and of itself. Just like a picture of your family or friends represents the love and commitment you have for each other."

"Yes: loving money is loving a photo of your family. Loving your value is loving your family."

Joe's face softened. "I feel emotional right now, and I have no idea of why."

"Try this on: it's about expanding how you can love in a way that brings rapport to you, your relationships, and your wealth."

"Oh... that feels..." Joe's eyes darted away from Money as his eyes moistened. He stood up and carefully put his empty bowl in the sink. While Joe rummaged around in the fridge looking for another can of soda, Money stood in the kitchen doorway without saying a word while the sounds of midday traffic drifted in through the half-open window.

Sidestepping Money, Joe dropped into his desk chair. He spun around a few times, feeling relief from the distraction. Then he stopped suddenly, seeing a higher moral ground argument. "At the end of the day, wouldn't it be better to simply share?"

"Many wealthy families set up charities and nonprofits."

"But they still shower themselves with one-hundred-dollar bills while gloating amidst the misery of humanity."

"That's a very concise description of the misery model of money. Not only does this bias not serve current humanity, but it also isn't serving future generations, either."

"What are you saying about future generations?"

"Let's talk about capital accumulation."

"If you're going to lecture me about the beneficial aspects of excess wealth, fair warning: Pissed may show up."

"Pissed is the perfect voice to challenge what I'm going to say next."

"Your positive reframes aren't going to change the impact of wealth inequality. Wouldn't it be better just to redistribute all this excess?"

"If wealthy people have accumulated a big bunch of Certificates of Appreciation by adding value to others, then—as often happens—most wealthy people reach out and multiply the value they've created. By collecting a big pile of Certificates of Appreciation, the wealthy can think further into the future. For example, let's say you have only five dollars in your pocket, and you're hungry. What do you do?"

"I buy something to eat."

"Now, let's say that you have ten million dollars in your pocket. What do you do?"

"Buy something with bigger pockets?" Joe laughed, then shook his head. "I can't even imagine it."

"Imagine you earned those certificates by creating a new technology for organic farming. This technology brings down the price of organic produce, so more people can enjoy it. Not only have you added value to a lot of people, but you also have ten million Certificates of Appreciation in the bank. What do you do?"

"Give it away to those in need?"

"Great. Let's say you give away half and keep five million in the bank. Now what do you do?"

"I don't know."

"There's a reason you don't know. Let me script a movie your mind can see. The main character is a creative engineer who solved some tough problems and created a product that made your life easier, and made her wealthy. Does she spend it all on food?"

"Of course not."

"As part of building a business, she also acquired knowledge, skills, productive behaviors, and beliefs about herself and the world that proved effective. She not only has talent, but is comfortable with success. She no longer needs to worry about her financial future and can start thinking about her kids and grandkids. She can think about big, complex projects that take time. Her capital can now benefit the human race in the long term."

"Theory, Money. Just theory."

"If everyone has only five dollars in their pockets, we would only consume the available food—and even the seeds. If we all had a million dollars in our pockets, we could invest in the future well-being of our communities."

"Come on, Money. The guy who uses his extra scratch to plant an orchard isn't thinking about the welfare of future generations. He's thinking about how much money he can make selling peaches."

"Now for the reframe. Ready?"

"Oh God, here it comes..."

"Depending on the person, they may very well focus on how much money they can make in the long term. They may also be motivated by how their children can carry on the business and add even more value to that orchard. The motivations are many."

"And the reframe?"

"Without capital, there can't be any concern for the future at all. There will be no orchards. Motivations don't matter."

"I don't care how many peach trees they plant. I still don't want to live in a world where rich people have all the money and are constantly screwing over little guys like me!"

Money smiled. "I see Pissed has arrived."

Joe just glared, affirming Money's observation. "We can tax the rich and distribute it to those in need."

"Let's back up to where we agree, shall we? You said you prefer to live in a world where some people have enough capital to invest in the future."

"No, I said I didn't want to live in a world where everybody was hungry with just five dollars in their pockets. It's valid to have resources for R&D, but they shouldn't be in the hands of capricious individuals."

"So, let's remove R&D investment decisions from capricious individuals and create a power structure that uses force to prevent investment decisions that don't conform. Remember our discussion—money or power? You can't eliminate capricious individuals without creating capricious power."

Joe opened and closed his mouth, unable to formulate a proper objection.

"I made a reframe and turned your negative into a positive, which caused you some discomfort. Your subconscious, or the voice you call Pissed, feels threatened because it doesn't know if this new world is safe and fair. Remember, any road we take runs in both directions. You can backtrack to Pissed's beliefs at any time. So, let's do a little experiment. Ready?"

Joe paused, feeling rushed. After a moment, he took a deep breath and nodded.

"Great. Continue taking several deep breaths."

Joe took several deep breaths, each deeper and slower than the previous one.

"As an experiment, repeat this phrase: 'I prefer to live in a world where some people have excess capital to invest in the future.' Say it out loud, even if you don't mean it. Remember, this is just an experiment."

"I prefer to live in a world where some people have excess capital to invest in the future." Joe said the words quickly.

"Now, repeat it slowly, and imagine that you mean it."

Joe repeated the words, but this time he allowed himself to feel the impact.

"Now, bring your awareness to your physical sensations. What's going on?"

"I feel a huge charge throughout my body. It's the same feeling as when I went on vacation several years ago. It's like anticipation, but also not knowing what's going to happen."

"Good. What feelings are present?"

"I feel giddy."

"Now, take a moment and notice what thoughts are coming and going through your head."

"I think I'm crazy! Why should repeating a simple sentence make me feel the way I do?"

"I've mentioned the discomfort you will experience during our conversations, but I didn't tell you about the potential exhilaration. As we start to make some breakthroughs, you'll experience this exhilaration many times over. You're now aware in real time of a shift in the context of your world. As we discussed, immediate awareness of these shifts is the first step in choosing the quality of your world and your life."

"Yes, but why do I still have the old anger? Why does Pissed still say that capitalism is exploitation?"

"People have the idea that transformation happens linearly, but that isn't how it works. You've immersed your life in social justice. You have strong empathetic feelings for those who suffer. You have absorbed this struggle, and it feels like it is part of who you are at the core. As you step into a new world with a new context, you still have all those existing triggers from your past. That is why we come back to the Golden Keys: Awareness, Acceptance, and Asking for what we want next."

"But if I accept new responses, won't they take over at some point?"

"Pissed and other voices will still show up from time to time. We can appreciate the old gang being there, and use these opportunities to learn and grow."

Capital for a Better Future —
For our Children

Issue: With the cultural pressure to define fairness as equality of outcome, we can adopt both conscious and subconscious negative beliefs about wealth. These beliefs come from a place of positive intention and can also anchor or sabotage our wealth opportunities.

Exercise Description: Do a baseline awareness check of your sensations, emotions, and thoughts and write them down. Then repeat a specific sentence out loud. Do another awareness check and compare the results to the baseline check. What was your experience as you said this sentence out loud? What physical sensations did you notice? What emotions came up? What thoughts went through your head?

Outcome: Raise your awareness of your visceral and emotional beliefs about capital accumulation and investment.

Time to Complete: 15 minutes

Prerequisites: None

Exercise Access: You will find detailed instructions in your complimentary online course.

Join or log into your complimentary online course here:

https://conversations.money/book-exercises/

Chapter 22 — Design: Cause or Effect?

J oe waited outside Julie's apartment, killing time while she got ready. He'd taken a gamble, signed up for a pair of free tickets to a panel talk about design, and texted Julie earlier that week. The way they'd ended their last date had left him nervous and out of sorts, but Julie accepted his olive branch offer.

Joe had already entered the university lecture hall's address into the rideshare app, so it only took one click to confirm the ride. Julie made only brief eye contact as she greeted him. "Nice to see you, Joe." They reached the curb just as the Lyft driver turned onto the street and came down the block, windshield signage glowing. Julie got in the back seat and slid over, and Joe quickly followed. "I know design isn't your thing," Julie said, "so I appreciate you thinking of me."

"It was on my event app and had your name all over it."

"But not yours."

"Yeah."

Dense traffic turned a ten-minute ride into thirty, but it may as well have been an hour as far as Joe was concerned. They managed some small talk, but he keenly felt the stiffness between them.

Joe displayed the virtual tickets on his phone, and they quickly stepped into the university auditorium vestibule, waiting for the doors to open. Recognizing a friend, Julie ran over and hugged an attractive man a little older than them. Two women her age quickly joined her, and they started an animated conversation. Unsure of himself, Joe walked over to the edge of the group.

Julie turned and said, "Joe, this is one of the city's best design pros, Peter Morgan. And these are my friends Pat and Barbara. Everyone, this is my, uh, friend, Joe."

As Joe shook hands, he straightened his posture to match Peter's stature.

The doors opened, and the noisy crowd moved into the small auditorium. Julie grabbed the arms of her two friends, and they found seats together. Joe followed and took a seat next to Julie. The animated conversation among the women continued without Joe, who found himself regretting the decision to set up this date.

The president of the organization president soon took the stage. She was slightly nervous and spoke rapidly and at length, but finally got things rolling.

Two hours later, even Joe had to admit the panel talk was fascinating. The speaker gave many examples of how our internal mental constructs reflect the environments that we create for ourselves. The theories proposed were interesting and thought-provoking.

The lecture ended with polite applause. Julie hugged Pat and Barbara passionately and slowly, and Joe saw her capacity for warmth. He then felt a pang of jealousy. He realized this was the first time he had seen her with other people, and he had missed a big part of her personality. Her warmth was so intoxicating that he felt a flutter of anticipation, which quickly turned sensual. The feeling was so intense that he shut it down.

Joe's new habit of taking a deep breath kicked in as soon as he noticed his internal critic stabbing him in the stomach. He allowed himself to stay with the feelings and inner voices as they came and went.

"What did you think of the event?" Joe asked as soon as he and Julie were settled into the Lyft back to Julie's neighborhood.

"What fascinates me is the potential to create designs and environments that impact every aspect of our being. For example, when we step into a sterile office building, we know how to behave and what to do, and it gives us a certain feeling. Or, if we step into a lover's bedroom, that is a very different context, with all the associated hormonal brain chemistry and physiological responses. In each of those contexts, other context may not even be available."

Joe got a physical rush thinking about Julie's bedroom comment, and it took a moment to come back to what she'd said. "Yeah... You know, I grew up as an evangelical. When I went to church, that context held almost everything—I mean, what I believed about the world, metaphysics, epistemology, ethics, beliefs, and behaviors. When I went to church, I knew all the hymns. I knew how to behave in every respect. In that context, it would've been impossible..." Joe thought about what he was saying, testing its veracity. "... Yes, impossible to be aware of other contexts. So, can design create a more hospitable or productive context?"

Julie looked out the window. Joe hoped she was lost in thought and not withdrawing.

"Stop here."

The driver turned with raised eyebrows.

"Please just pull over in front of the coffee shop on the right." Julie turned to Joe. "I appreciate the tickets. Can I buy you a cup of coffee? There's a lot to think and talk about."

Joe felt his heart beat faster, but decided to cover his nervousness with a joke. "As long as it's free, why not?"

"Nothing's free, Joe. There's always a price." Then she smiled.

152

Chapter 23 — Transmutation: Turning Lead into Gold

"i feel your presence, money. you seem to know when it's time to talk again."

"you've come a long way since your nightmares. i want to acknowledge your progress from being your reactions to observing those reactions from the perspective of your higher self."

"i'm not sure what's happening, but i certainly feel different." joe laughed. "it's weird, but i feel more comfortable with an apparition now than i do with humans."

"may i reframe that, joe?"

joe grinned. "what a surprise!"

"try saying this: 'it's bizarre, but i feel safer with myself and who i am.'"

"okay: 'i feel safer with myself and who i am.'"

"how does that feel?"

"i feel my face flush and tingles in my fingertips."

"please appreciate your ability to be aware of your sensations and feelings in real time. i can't emphasize enough how this expanding ability supports the new beliefs, behaviors, and outcomes that you want."

"yes, i can observe these sensations and feelings and not be terrified. this is so unlike me."

"another reframe?"

"Of course."

" 'This used to be so unlike me. I'm now eager to test new ways of experiencing myself to see what works better for me.' "

Joe repeated the new reframe without hesitation.

"What was that like?"

"Exciting and scary."

"Now that you're so eager to test new ways of experiencing yourself, how about we turn some lead into gold?"

"Can you turn lead into gold? If so, you can make everybody rich!"

"This is exactly the conversation I want to have today: what makes wealth? Joe, a thought experiment?"

Joe nodded in agreement.

"Let's imagine that I turned lead into gold and gave everyone in the world as much as they could carry. Now, with your many years of understanding how humans behave, tell me what might happen?"

"I can tell you what I would do. I'd buy a nice house and get out of this ratty apartment. I'd buy a new car and travel. And I could take Julie on very nice dates."

"Terrific. What if every 'Joe' in the world decided to do the same thing?"

"Okay... we're all having a great time, and there is a lot less suffering."

"Now let's imagine that every 'Joe' in the world decided to buy a new house, all at the same time."

Joe's brow wrinkled. "Gosh. There wouldn't be enough houses on the market."

"What happens to the price of houses?"

"I guess if everyone came with a suitcase of gold to buy a new house, the sellers would just ask for more gold."

"Exactly right. If no one builds houses, then no new value is created. Nobody would be better off. So, here's the crux of it, Joe; here is the critical point. Money is not wealth. I am not wealth."

Joe's eyes met Money's, and he continued to hold eye contact. "But money *is* wealth."

"Having more money, without creating more value, does not improve our lives. Do you remember our conversation about Certificates of Appreciation?"

"Of course I do."

"Certificates of Appreciation represent the value that is delivered. If you just print money without delivering value, then nobody is better off."

"But some people are better off."

"Yes; when a counterfeiter or government prints money, they're able to *extract* value from others without *delivering* corresponding value. The extra dollars in circulation devalue everybody's Certificates of Appreciation by some tiny amount. Thus, a counterfeiter is stealing money from everyone who has saved money for the future. Joe, remember that I have had a lot of experience over the centuries with governments and money. There are very few examples of governments who have not used their money-printing presses to buy approval and keep themselves in power. It's just too easy and far too tempting. As a result, when governments manufacture more money, they're stealing from people who have created and delivered value."

"But the government has a targeted inflation rate that stimulates the economy and balances employment."

"Ah, Modern Monetary Theory. Speaking as the final authority on money, I can state unequivocally that the theory is a meaningless, complex mental contortion—a string of important-sounding words that, when broken down, have no real meaning. Economic philosophy isn't a complex academic study. Here is economics in one sentence—"

"You're going to dismiss the entire academic field of economics in one sentence?"

"Even worse: how about in one word? Ready?"

"I think you've already given it away."

"Yes, as a *personal* mindset. But it also applies to economics. Think of the word as a unified theory of everything money."

" 'Value'?"

"Yes. 'Value.' The best economic systems incentivize people to produce the most value, given humanity's fallible nature. Good economics is about understanding this dynamic in detail. The more value, the more wealth. Period."

"So, doesn't that make you not very important?"

"Bingo. I'm only important when used as a comparative measure of value. What if, just imagine for a moment, you woke up tomorrow, and your only thought was, *How can I deliver value to those around me?*"

"You mean figuring out how to deliver value to my publishers? Most of them are pricks."

"On some level, do you think that your publishers pick up on that attitude?"

"I think I hide it pretty well... but I do notice it when other people are hiding something from me."

"So, what if you spent the next week engaged in creatively thinking about how you can deliver more value to your publishers? What if you were to approach your publishers, editors, readers, and everyone you know with your desire to deliver value?"

"If I were to have an attitude like that, they'd take advantage of it."

"Yes, indeed. But for now, assume you're capable of setting boundaries that honor yourself. With this mindset, you can fully, with all your heart, deliver value to your magazine editors."

"This makes me realize how conflicted I am. Pissed doesn't want to give those jerks the satisfaction."

"So, do you see how your attitude contributes to your current outcomes?"

"I'm afraid if I don't punch first, I'll get hurt again."

"This is an important point. *We don't change our beliefs or behaviors without a more positive alternative.* We only move towards new beliefs and behaviors when our survival mechanism gives us the okay."

"You were going to talk about turning lead into gold. I don't get it."

"Delivering value is like gold. The more we learn how to deliver the highest-quality value, the purer the gold we create."

"But what if others are not interested in the value we offer?"

"Then it's not of value to them. It's that simple."

"You want me to measure value from the recipient's point of view. But what if my value system is different? This is so complex."

Money laughed. "We'll break it down later. In the meantime, I have an exercise that I'll email to you. With some focus, it'll help you discover what value you might lose with wealth."

"How could I lose value if I have more wealth?"

"This is a counterintuitive exercise. Of course, your brain will resist, but I have faith that you'll make some discoveries."

"Do you appreciate how much turmoil I feel? I'm on a roller coaster that goes from anticipation and curiosity to holy terror cascading into the unknown."

"Yes, indeed. Enjoy the ride! Later, Joe."

"Later, Money."

Chapter 24 — Designing the Relationship

The sandwich shop bustled with the lunchtime crowd. When Julie spotted Joe, she automatically started on his order, and it was ready to go when he got to the front of the line. He handed her the exact amount of money, allowing her hand to rest on his.

"The place is hopping today!"

"I'll say!" Julie said over the din. "How about someplace quiet for dinner?"

"Huh?" Joe said, surprised.

"My place. I'll cook."

Joe turned, and a young man waiting for pastrami on rye gave him a thumbs-up. Joe's face turned beet red.

The bus down Geary Boulevard was ten minutes late, but Joe wasn't worried. He had built time into his route to compensate for the possibility. As the bus thundered along, he was careful to keep a good grip on the midrange wine he was carrying.

Thankfully, Joe arrived ten minutes early. Once Julie let him in, he removed his backpack and placed the wine on her beautifully arranged table, thinking about their nighttime conversation in the coffee shop. They had spent two hours talking about design, and Joe could now see evidence of Julie's talent throughout her apartment.

He couldn't remember being in a place that was so distinctive and yet harmonious.

Explaining that it would be about half an hour before the chicken tikka masala was out of the oven, Julie lightly took Joe's arm and settled him into a well-worn couch. She brought him sparkling water without asking and sat in the matching upholstered chair opposite him.

Joe took some time to look around the apartment. "I now understand what you mean about designing spaces better."

"You mean, you understand better, or I design spaces better?"

"Both."

Julie laughed with Joe, tucked one long leg up under her flowing blue skirt, and rested her chin on her knee with grace and ease.

"I like to spend time at flea markets, used furniture stores, Goodwill, even pawnshops. I love discovering things that fill a space and fit in just right."

Joe took a big gulp of his sparkling water. Julie blushed and quickly exited for the kitchen to check on the Indian dish.

Joe walked over to the table. He pulled a corkscrew out of his backpack, opened the wine, and poured half a glass for each of them, taking a glass to Julie. She took a sip and stirred the wild rice. There seemed to be an implicit agreement that an awkward conversation needed to start. Julie turned to Joe, and both started at once.

Julie laughed. "You go."

"Ladies first."

"Alright, I'm going to be honest, and I don't want anything less from you. I realize we both have demons, triggers, and strong feelings. I'm working hard to create the life I want, and your attitude in the park upset me. You were too sharp for me. But when you invited me to the event, I realized that I was the one being defensive.

I invited you here to have a conversation that's both honest and open."

Joe managed to hold eye contact with Julie while letting her words sink in. He quickly checked his physical sensations and noticed his rapid heartbeat and tight chest.

Julie leaned forward, almost imperceptibly, but the impact was powerful.

"You want honesty?" he asked. "A big part of me is ringing the alarms and wants to shut you out."

Julie moved back an inch. "I appreciate knowing that. And if that's what you need to do, I'll accept that."

"No!" Joe roared as he set his glass on the counter. "No," he added softly. He briefly thought about Money and the reframes he had survived. Here, looking him directly in the eyes, was an invitation to step into a world he was afraid of—and craved at the same time.

After a long look at Joe's face, seeking a clue to the commitment behind the 'no,' Julie responded, "I need to talk about my personal freedom and what that means..."

After her long and tearful explanation, Joe realized their relationship couldn't be defined by his own needs and expectations as Julie revealed her fear of being saddled.

Once again, it was the dock or the canoe. He took the risk with awareness and reached for Julie. She opened her arms, accepting his embrace.

Chapter 25 — Money's Rules

"**G**lad you're back." Joe turned on the stained coffee pot without looking at Money. "The roller coaster has come off its tracks."

"Excellent! For clarity, let's define the tracks you are leaving and the new tracks you're taking."

"That's the problem. I don't see new tracks, only a black void."

"You've clearly described the emotional sensation of making a change, even one that may serve you better. Your old beliefs and behaviors are like the tracks for a toy train that just goes around in circles. It sounds like you're ready to jump those tracks. And, as we've discussed, your survival brain won't let you go anywhere that hasn't been certified as safe. So, let's create a new set of tracks. Imagine these new tracks as principles that not only feel better, but are based on your core values and in alignment with your goals."

"Principles about what?"

"Principles about money. These principles will help establish new tracks that'll serve you better."

After twenty minutes of conversing in the now-familiar question-and-answer style, they worked up two foundational statements. Money referred to them as "the rules"—but rules created to support Joe's highest values.

"Let me clarify our messy language and state them in positive language," Money said. "First, all transactions involving money are voluntary and exclude the use or threat of force. Second, all transactions involving money are fully transparent and honest. Are you okay with these rules?"

Joe considered the clarification for a moment, looking for the trap he felt must be there. "They sound good. But I reserve the right to back up to my old track if needed."

"Absolutely. Now, let's talk about delivering value."

"I think we've beaten that horse enough."

"We aren't beating horses. We're doing the opposite. As you know, delivering value is a complex process with many diverse people involved. If you goal is to deliver value, the question arises—"

"Oh, I see," Joe interrupted. "With everyone having different values and they also value goods and services differently, how do we determine *whose* values?"

"Excellent, and this needs clarity. When we deliver value, we deliver value as measured by the person who receives it, not by the person who delivers it. Does that make sense?"

Joe took a sip of coffee. "I'm okay with using that as a working assumption for now."

"This may help you with that assumption. Because all transactions are voluntary, you never have to deal with a transaction you feel would harm somebody else. In other words, nobody can force you to become a drug dealer."

"What a relief," Joe said sarcastically. "So, if I understand correctly, all parties in the transaction can follow their personal value system and determine which transactions they want to make or not make. Does that describe the model?"

"I think that gives us the third rule, no?" Money said.

Joe nodded.

Money grabbed a notebook from Joe's desk and jotted down the following:

1. *All monetary transactions are voluntary and exclude the use or threat of force.*

2. *All transactions are transparent and honest.*

3. *Each individual determines the value of every transaction for themselves.*

Joe felt Pissed's energy erupting, and at that moment he had no desire to tamp it down. "These rules might make sense for a simple transaction, like buying a used TV on eBay. But taking a minimum-wage job is different. Accepting a minimum-wage job might look consensual, transparent, and honest on the surface, but in reality, it isn't. Young people may be able to live on that pay now, but they'll be left in dire straits by middle age. Many people can't find better jobs, so they're forced to take bad jobs. Consent isn't possible if you can't choose. The system slams doors in your face."

Money allowed the full impact of Pissed's voice to fill the room before repeating Joe's last comment. " 'Consent isn't possible if you can't choose'?"

"Say some young person has to take the only job available to them. It's the only choice they have. They may not even know that the job is a dead end, and they'll end up with nothing but poverty in old age."

"Does anyone of any age know all the facts? Does one choice preclude making different choices later?"

"Of course not. You're distorting my point."

"How so?"

"The system doesn't teach people how to make good decisions. It doesn't teach people how to succeed."

"So, you would like a system that invites everyone to increase their ability to add value to their community and gain financial security?"

Joe glared at Money as he continued.

"Be careful here, Joe. Implicit in what you said was this: *some people are not capable of taking care of themselves.* That belief is a major fork in the road."

"They can't take care of themselves because of the system, not because they aren't capable."

"So, what you want is to give those capable people the ability to make a good life for themselves? Joe, this may sound strange, but I think you are slowly creating clarity from the fog. *You may not realize it, but you are creating clarity for your future self, the values you hold, and your life's mission.*"

Joe started to respond, then tightened his lips.

"Yes, Joe: your life's mission."

Joe closed his eyes, as if to sort out the words Money had just put in his mouth. "When I tell you about the beliefs I've had all my life, and you reframe them, there is a part of me that sees something I haven't seen before. But then Pissed starts screaming inside my head."

"Understood. So many books on making money, financial security, careers, and investing don't appreciate that it's the mindset shift that really matters and is foundational to opening all these doors. When you write your book—"

"—that you keep harping on..."

"Yes, when you write the book that I keep harping on, you'll give people an invitation to build a solid foundation of beliefs rather than just dealing with symptoms financial stress."

After Money left, Joe decided to take stock of all he'd learned since their first conversation. Determined not to overthink it, he turned to a fresh page in his notebook and quickly started writing. Ten minutes later, he stared at a list that included intellectual discoveries, new beliefs, and ongoing practices. The list was a full page long.

Joe sat there for a moment, taking it in. *These are accomplishments*, he thought. He couldn't deny that he'd made some amazing shifts. The list included clarity on his conflicting relationship with money and the Pissed part of himself, increasing self-awareness and acceptance, and reframing money from being the "root of all evil" to Certificates of Appreciation for value delivered.

Chapter 26 — Owning Your Success Thermostat

J oe stood on his tiptoes. For all its faults, the warehouse space that had been renovated into his apartment had a high ceiling making him stretch to reach the very top of the upper window pane. Once done cleaning it, he sprayed more window cleaner on his rag and moved over to the next pane.

Sitting quietly at the bistro table, Money watched him work.

Joe stepped back for a second to see the impact of his efforts. "That does make a big difference, doesn't it?"

"Yes, indeed. Sometimes it's the small things that matter."

"I wanted to clean the windows when I first moved in, but I put it off for so long, I forgot about it. Actually, it's not so much that I for-got about it; it's more like I couldn't see them anymore, or at least how dirty they really were."

"Humans have a fascinating ability to be blind to what's right in front of them in order to preserve their beliefs."

"That describes Julie."

"How so?"

"Well, she may be a conservative, or at least a capitalist."

"And from that position, what is her blind spot?"

"She thinks everyone can pull themselves up by their bootstraps."

"Did she actually say, 'Everyone can pull themselves up by their bootstraps'?"

"Well, not in so many words."

"Here is your own blind spot, Joe. In order to make her wrong from your own perspective, you exaggerate her comments to make her seem unfeeling. That allows you to be right."

Joe started to reply reactively, then paused and took a breath, remaining silent.

"Julie is determined not to just passively dream like her mother, but to work to gain the skills she needs," Money went on. "However, this is a fragile belief she is putting into place, and it is easily shaken because she fears being like her mom."

"So, when she attacked my articles by saying they were like a dream, or like her mom's vision boards, that lit my fuse."

"Exactly. And what did the fuse light off?"

Joe snorted, then laughed. "It's not funny, but..."

"But?"

"If I look at my articles, they *are* a vision board—not a vision of wealth or success, but a vision of how everyone is *not* supposed to operate."

"By whose rules?"

Joe laughed again. "By my rules!"

"And what does that do for you, if everyone obeys your rules?"

"This is what isn't funny." Joe looked at the floor for guidance, and found none.

Money's soft gaze waited for Joe's eyes to return. The silence felt like an eternity to Joe.

"It means I don't have to look at my own blind spots." Joe paused. "There, I said it."

"And now that you are cleaning your windows, what is your blind spot?"

"That I can seem righteous just by criticizing the system—and I don't have to actually do anything. I guess Julie had a point; maybe I am like her mom." Joe shook his head. "But she also said that there is something too intimate to share with me."

"That must be confusing."

"More than that—it's terrifying." Mulling this over, Joe moved to the next windowpane, shifting the blinds and wincing at the sudden influx of light.

"You know, Money," he said as he started scrubbing, "I think Julie isn't the only one in my life engaged in a fear-based relationship with you."

"Who do you have in mind?"

"Ian. He and Julie couldn't be more different, but fear is there in both cases. Julie is scared she's going to make the same borrowing mistake twice, or be like her mom. Ian is scared that any little bit of money he gets is going to get taken away. He was told that his budget for freelancers was going to increase, but he didn't believe it. And the same thing happened when the magazine signed a big new advertising contract; he actually thought he'd get laid off. It's like Julie can't 'pass Go and collect two hundred dollars,' while Ian is worried that every time he passes Go, he will 'go directly to jail,' and that two hundred dollars will be taken away."

"So, Julie is once bitten, twice shy, and Ian is waiting for the other shoe to drop?"

Joe smiled. 'Two clichés in one sentence that sum up what I said! Maybe *you* should write the book."

"I would, but I don't need the money."

Joe laughed.

"Joe, this is important: for both Ian and Julie, fear is the driver, even if the symptoms are different."

Joe looked out the remaining dirty windowpane as the word "fear" hung in the air.

"And Joe's fear?" Money asked

Once again, Joe's eyes returned to the linoleum floor for guidance before he spoke. "Crap..." Money honored the silence that followed. "Crap."

" 'Crap'?" Money's eyebrows raised.

"Yeah, crap. The fear is that Joe," he said, pointing to his chest, "is afraid he'll become one of *them*."

Joe put the spray cleaner on the table, finished with the task. "You know," he said, "as long as my windows were dirty, I didn't have to take responsibility for what I couldn't see—and it's like that with wealth. If I'm poor, I can be righteous and blame the system. Whereas if I'm wealthy, I have to make decisions that impact a lot of people. I could do real damage."

Money leaned forward, appreciating this turn in the conversation. "How have you maintained these conflicts?"

"So far, I've avoided it. But in the future, I'm going to have to take risks that could impact other people."

"How is that a problem?"

"Isn't it self-evident? I could make a visible public mistake."

"And if you did?"

"Money! Isn't that enough?"

"No, it's not enough. We're close to a core truth. What if you did make a public mistake?"

Joe turned and looked through the clean window, noticing how foreign the world looked. "I'm not capable of handling wealth."

"So in addition to your guilt, you have fear?"

Joe nodded. "I feel so small right now, like I'm not worthy."

"Allow yourself to feel small. In fact, exaggerate and think the thoughts that make you smaller."

Joe sat on the worn couch and bent forward with his arms wrapped tightly around his chest, still gripping the cleaning rag. "From where I am now, I'm not sure I even know the meaning of the word *wealth*."

"This is a magical moment, Joe. You can stay with the feeling, and at the same time, continue to move forward with an exercise. To make this easier, imagine you have a twin who is just like you, except his worthiness isn't even in question. He holds his head up high and has the right to walk on this earth. Can you imagine your twin?"

"Hard to do when I don't feel it myself."

"Stand up and move to this corner."

Joe followed Money's instructions.

"In this corner, you are the worthy twin. You are worthy of wealth and success. You are proud of the Certificates of Appreciation you have accumulated. You learn from the feedback you receive for your actions, and are eager to learn more. You survey the world in front of you and see so many opportunities to add value. With this mind-set, how would your posture change?"

Joe stood up straight, shoulders back, and took a deep breath. He held eye contact with Money. Slowly his body and mind took on the characteristics of his imagined twin.

"Now, when you're ready, describe your wealthy self in vivid detail. Take all the time you need."

With his hands clasped behind his back, Joe strolled to the window as his shoulders slumped, unable to maintain the persona of his twin. "I keep making excuses to justify being rich—like living fairly simply, so no one will know."

"Exactly right. By doing this exercise, you'll discover all the tricks your survival mechanism has used to keep you safe by maintaining your struggle. Your struggle itself is your safety. If you're worthy, you're not only able to handle money and wealth, but you're able to learn from your mistakes."

"What if the money goes to my head, and I can't handle wealth?"

"Notice when I asked you to take on the persona of your wealthy twin, you were unable to hold it. Step back into the corner and play a new movie in your head. What if the main character learned from his mistakes, and learned to handle wealth elegantly?"

Joe shivered as an image of elegant wealth formed in his mind. "That movie didn't exist ten seconds ago. Now that it's in my head, it feels intense, almost painful."

"Learning to handle wealth is so intense for most people that they maintain behaviors that repeat the same failing patterns. However, I'm here to invite you to your new movie and let you know that those intense feelings are okay. In fact, they're the precursors of powerful new beliefs."

Joe laughed. "It never ends, does it? Just like the poster says, it's the journey, not the destination."

"It's both. On the journey, you develop processes that create outcomes. You check the outcomes, then adjust the processes, back and forth. And I do have an exercise to increase your awareness of your 'wealth thermostat.' "

"Can I grab lunch first?"

Money grinned. "No worries. I'll send it in an email."

Wealth Identity Exercise

Issue: Most people are content with their life trajectory, income group, and retirement status. As a result, their behaviors will support that comfort zone. Some people dream big and never succeed. Others have developed a process for their lives that gives them an excellent chance of changing their financial status.

Exercise Description: This exercise sharpens your observation of people whose identity, beliefs, and behaviors create a known, limited outcome. Others in your life have developed processes that improve their "skill stack" and are willing to learn, grow, test, fail, and succeed.

Outcome: Create your list of factors for both stasis and growth, and look at yourself through that filter.

Time to Complete: 20–30 minutes

Prerequisites: None

Exercise Access: You will find detailed instructions in your complimentary online course.

Join or log into your complimentary online course here:
https://conversations.money/book-exercises/

Chapter 27 — Welcome to the Galactic Wormhole

J ulie's apartment became the eye of Joe's emotional hurricane. It symbolized everything he longed for, and everything he could lose. Every time he opened the door, he maintained the habit of taking a deep breath as he felt the intimacy of stepping into an extension of Julie herself. He conflated the apartment with the woman who lived there in a way he could not untangle.

Joe set the Chinese takeout on the small table and moved to the open window, which overlooked a small park and miles of apartments and houses. "Your windows are always clean."

Julie appeared beside him and put her arm around his waist while looking out the window with him. "Are you calling me obsessive?"

"I love your clean windows! I love how your apartment feels. I love the conversations we've had, even though some of them were difficult."

Joe talked more about his experience while Julie set the table. She put the food into big, colorful serving bowls and placed chopsticks next to each plate.

"Thank you for letting me know all of that," she said as she took her seat.

Joe sat down across from her. "Among all the agreements we've made," he continued, "the most difficult has been total honesty. I've always used clever language to, uh..." Ironically, he struggled to find the right words.

Julie maintained eye contact without needing to rescue him.

"... I've always manipulated what I've said to please others, while at the same time hiding what I feel. Part of me is fearful I'll never find someone like you again, and that part wants to be very careful and not say anything that upsets you. I'm putting everything on the line. If it doesn't work..."

"If it doesn't work?" Julie prompted.

"If it doesn't work, I'm willing to feel the pain."

Julie reached across the table and lightly touched Joe's hand. "I knew from the moment I made that first chicken salad sandwich that you were going to take a big bite out of my heart."

Joe blinked, unsure how to take this, and Julie burst into laughter at his rattled look. Joe joined in, happy to put their electricity on the back burner and just enjoy being silly together.

"I have some good news," Julie said. "Remember Peter Connor?"

"The guy from the design talk?"

"That's the one. Peter and I keep in touch via the online design community."

Joe instantly noticed a pang of jealousy and suspicion, but took a breath and let it go. He was pleased that he could catch old movies and patterns in real time and release them.

"Anyhow, I don't remember how it came up, but I mentioned the thing about Certificates of Appreciation. He asked where I got the idea, and I told him it was from you. He liked the idea so much, he mentioned it to a friend who's an editor at an educational magazine with a big online following. Her name is Maria Elena, and Peter said that she'd like you to call her about doing an article. I'll text you her info. Peter also said that when you talk to her, ask Maria Elena about Bala."

Joe looked perplexed, and Julie shrugged. "You might not want to work with her, but it doesn't hurt to find out."

Joe's forehead wrinkled. "Interesting. I've been documenting as much as I can of all my conversations with Money."

"Money?"

"You know, uh, that friend I met online... uh... through an email." Joe quickly took a sip of tea. He hadn't exactly lied, but it bumped up against his promise to be honest. "I have no idea what this Bala thing could be, but a lot of what's coming from Money could make a great article."

Julie smiled shyly. "Maybe even a book!"

Joe's head jerked up. "Oh no—not you, too! Money's always pushing me to write a book."

"It seems you can't get away from your friend Money."

"Believe me, I've tried!... Alright, a book it is. You can only fight the universe for so long."

"If it's just Money and me that you're fighting, it's a pretty small universe."

Joe laughed, unsure whether the universe was truly small, or if Julie and Money were gatekeepers to the galactic wormhole of all his futures.

Chapter 28 — Don't Eat the Whole Pie

"Hey, Joe. Wake up."

Joe pulled the blankets over his head. "Go away."

"I made coffee. My special blend."

"I'm not going to think about new things."

"Okay, no problem. The coffee is ready when you are."

"As long as I don't have to think about any new things."

"Agreed."

Joe peeked one eye out from the covers. "You're lying."

"Well... only because I want to gain your trust before we think of new things."

"Yeah, good strategy. Don't you ever let up?"

"Hmmm... let me think." Money mimed a thoughtful face. "Ah: NO."

"Okay, just give me twenty minutes to shower. That is, if the damn water heater works."

While washing his hair, Joe cringed at the thought of stepping into Money's intellectual whirlwind so early in the morning. He stayed in the shower long enough to start waking up, then the water turned shockingly cold, completing the wake-up job. Money poured a cup of coffee as Joe entered the kitchen, fully awake. Joe sat down and warmed his hands on the hot mug before taking a sip. "Good coffee," he said.

"Glad you like it. Now let's review the assumptions we made."

"Can we skip the review?"

"I want to be sure we're clear on every assumption. If transactions are voluntary, why, of your own free will, would you make a transaction using money?"

"To gain something I wanted."

"Yes, and you're willing to part with money to get it."

"Right. The money I give is worth less to me than the value I receive."

"What about the other person in the transaction?"

"Well, they'd value the money more than the product or service they delivered."

"And why would they prefer the money?"

"Because they know they can approach someone else and offer them that money for a product or service that *they* want."

"Excellent. So far, all parties are satisfied and have added value to others. Agreed?"

Joe nodded.

"So, what role did I play as money?"

"Well, it's a bit complicated to think it through. You were a measure of value. You represented some value I created for another person. I could then transfer that value to someone completely different. That person who received the money could take that representation of value and exchange it for value from someone else."

"Yes: a proxy for value. Now, let's expand this concept and apply it to the thought that someone has to lose."

"Uh-oh," Joe said. "I hear Pissed approaching. He just dropped in to say that there's only so much money in the world, and those who grab the most are bogarting it."

"Thank you, Pissed, for that clarity. Your 'one pie' economic model has been adopted by many, consciously or unconsciously. And they're right in the sense that there is a fixed amount of currency available at any given time. Unfortunately, this gives rise to the belief that we have limited wealth. But here's a better framework: is there a limit to the amount of value we can create and deliver to each other?"

Joe smiled. "Pissed went dark again, so I'll answer for him. No, there's no limit to the amount of value we can create."

"Well said. Many people apply the constraint of a limited supply of currency to the unlimited ability to create value. They think of wealth as 'thing,' not an expanding process of healthy human interaction. Thinking of wealth as a 'thing' is like thinking of a flowing river with its many sources as a frozen lake. Clarifying this confusion is critically important."

Joe rested his chin on his hands. "I can't believe what I'm thinking, but I'm going to say it anyway. We talked earlier about me being... well, gosh, this is hard to say. We talked about me being a good guy. When I say that, I feel uncomfortable. But, Money, it's true: I *am* a good guy. So, let me think this through aloud. If I'm a good guy, and if there is a fixed amount of money, I'm selfish if I accumulate money, because someone who is needier than me now has access to less. We started talking about pies, and now I'm not feeling worthy. This makes no sense."

"You're right, it doesn't make sense—but there is a connection. If you grew up in a world of 'not enough,' and you're selfish, you grab all you can. If you're good-hearted, you figure out who is worthy and deserves these limited resources. Combined with other messages, this makes it all too easy to believe we aren't worthy of wealth. Once we feel unworthy, every time we made money, a voice inside would say, 'You don't deserve this.' "

"Yeah, that feels..." Joe's voice trailed off as he stared into his now empty coffee cup.

"Feels what?"

"Too revealing!"

"Take all the time you need to allow yourself to notice."

"Sure," Joe said.

He didn't have to look up to know: Money was gone.

Joe stepped out of the kitchen and collapsed onto his bed. *Worthy*. The word echoed in his mind as he replayed significant events in his life through the lens of self-worth. After lying there for an hour, he sensed something started to gel. He moved to his computer, opened a new document, and started typing furiously, ignoring the grammar and spelling corrections.

You Aren't Worthy

There is only one pie. There are many people who want a big piece. You also want a big piece of pie, but you know in your heart you aren't worthy. There are other people far more deserving, far more worthy, who need the pie worse than you do.

You may not feel worthy for a number of reasons. Your parents may never have acknowledged your worth as a person. You may have shrunk yourself to avoid being competitive. Or it could even be that you work twice as hard as you need to, just to prove you're worthy, when underneath you know that you are not.

Whatever the reason, you don't feel like you deserve your place in the world as a human being. If at the same time, you believe the world has limited resources, limited money, and limited goods and services, where does this leave you? If you are undeserving and there are limited resources, then if you are a good person, your only choice is to shrink, get very small, and avoid competing for that piece of pie you want so badly. Meanwhile, watching everyone else gobble down their pie makes you feel resentful, angry, and excluded.

Is this the real world? If that's the world you're creating, yes. But if you create one where you're worthy and have a right to stand tall just like everybody else, the whole world becomes a very different place. It has an unlimited amount of value and cheers you on in your success.

I've lived in a one-pie universe and have felt unworthy all my life. The result has been living with a boiling anger that impacts everything I experience and do. It's not comfortable to step into the belief and knowing that I'm worthy and the world has an infinite amount of pie.

But what happens if I behave as if this were true?

I will keep you posted.

As soon as he finished writing this missive to himself, Joe opened his Google Docs folder labeled CwM. He then created a subfolder labeled Blog, his hands slightly shaking as he typed.

Chapter 29 — Values, Truth, and Reality

"**H**ello, Joe, whadaya know?" Money said playfully.

Joe smiled but immediately returned to washing the dishes, slightly preoccupied.

"You certainly look different," Money said.

Joe glanced over. If the fact that Money was wearing a tuxedo phased him, he didn't let on. "I *feel* different. Julie's professor introduced me to an editor at a new publication, and we started working together. The pay is better than at Themis, and we got off on the right foot. It feels like I'm finally creating a different movie in my mind."

"What a shift your mindset created!" Money said, loosening his bow tie and letting it hang.

"Are you saying my mindset changes others' behavior?"

"Let's find out!" Money grabbed Joe's notebook from the desk. He glanced at the list of accomplishments Joe had scribbled down and nodded. Then, without saying a word, Money flipped the page, finding the rules they had formulated together.

1. *All monetary transactions are voluntary and exclude the use or threat of force.*

2. *All transactions are transparent and honest.*

3. *Each individual determines the value of every transaction for themselves.*

"Did you force her to agree? Were you honest? Did she see value for herself?"

"Well, to the first point, it goes without saying that I can't use force with an editor. No pushing, no shoving. Next is the honesty part. That one's a little trickier, but I now realize how often I wrap up my resentment in 'nice' words. Frankly, Money, I'm amazed how much of my life is in continuous conflict."

"As you became aware of your inner world, you noticed a mismatch between the experience and your words?"

"I translate everything I say through a filter. Not sure what that filter is, but I'm becoming more aware of it."

"Excellent! With this awareness, are your conversations moving towards rapport with yourself and others?" Joe nodded, and Money grew quiet for a moment, then said in a burst, "So, let's focus on the third rule. Given our last conversation, what would it take for more Certificates of Appreciation to flow your way? We've discussed the theory; now let's move into specifics. Rather than convincing your editor to do something, you uncover what is valuable to her. Then you deliver value to her on her terms—is that right?"

"I have a general idea how to do this, but I've never thought about it in any real depth."

"Being open to stepping into someone else's shoes and understanding what they value is not a trivial skill. You may feel awkward at first, but if you dedicate yourself to delivering value to others on *their* terms, this intention alone allows you to see what you've never seen before. Your new skill will change your finances."

"You mean, like understanding what kind of pressure she's under, what her problems are, what solutions might work for her... ?"

"That's a great start."

Joe leaned back, closed his eyes, and spent several minutes in silence. "If I just even imagine focusing on *her* values, this is so different from my old world. It feels less like I'm struggling with her, but gaining rapport. This feeling is so different from being used and then feeling resentful and fighting for survival. Even though I covered my anger with 'nice guy' talk, I was still angry."

"And now?"

"Now it feels like, well, not completely changed, but there's a light in the fog."

"Excellent," Money said softly. "Very good, indeed. Now, I'm going to ask a very strange question."

Joe burst out laughing, leaving Money with a perplexed look on his face.

"Oh... yeah," Money said with a tiny laugh. "Well, this question is even stranger than the others." He cleared his throat, and Joe grinned. "Seriously, as you step into this new world of Certificates of Appreciation, delivering value to others, self-awareness, agency over your own feelings, an unlimited economy for everyone, our rules for money, and accumulated capital that contributes to the future for your children..."

"My children... ? Never mind, just get to the question."

"Joe, as you adopt this very different mindset, what of value do you stand to lose? Take your time with this."

It was Joe's turn to look perplexed. "Uh ...at this moment, it all looks good. There is nothing to lose."

"You attend events with other writers, journalists, and political advocates?"

"Yeah, that's where I see my friends."

"And I assume most of them agree with the tone of your articles and blog posts?"

"Well, yeah, we all feel pretty strongly about how the world can be made better. We see the current structures that are ossified by privilege, and that structure creates huge classes of victims that can't escape their fate." Joe started to speak again, then stopped abruptly, pursing his lips and looking down at the floor.

"How many times have you said that?"

Joe snorted. "Hundreds... maybe even thousands."

"Yeah, they sounded like a series of well-used words without much meaning. Could you clarify those words from the perspective of your emerging mindset?"

Joe opened his mouth, but no words came out.

"Now, Joe, imagine summarizing our conversations for a group at your next event. What would happen?"

"How should I know?"

"You know."

"Yeah, I know... I would get..."

"Get what?"

Joe's face darkened as he created the movie in his head. "It would get me... you know... canceled."

"And that would leave you... ?"

"Alone. I would be all alone."

"So, I'll ask the question again: what *of value* would you lose?"

Joe turned toward the one window and stepped in front of it. Money let that be without comment and sat down at the table. Then, after five minutes, without prompting, Joe rejoined Money.

"I would lose my entire world as I know it. Except maybe for maybe Julie." Joe buried his face in his hands. "Julie," he repeated, and started weeping.

Money waited until Joe was able to look up.

"Well done, Joe. You can stay with your feelings, even those that spring from a very deep well. And I have some good news."

"On my way to the guillotine, you tell me you have good news?" Joe laughed with a newly liberated deep voice, pounded the table, then laughed again.

"Yes: there is a new world of people that will find you attractive. These people are curious and want to learn, not just sing from the same hymnal. They think about the words they say, and ask others how they hear them. These people are proactive, and they take the initiative. They can do this because they are agents of their own lives, creating their own experiences and the world they want. They see the impact of their behavior and know how to change and adapt. They care about all people, not seeing them as a series of victims and perpetrators, but as growing agents in charge of their own lives. This mindset gives everyone around them a model and an invitation to a world that serves their values and goals. It is a model of rapport and responsibility, in the most positive sense of the word."

Joe shook his head. "That is a lot. I don't even think I can remember most of it. My brain wants to shut down."

"Understood. So, just remember this: humans are tribal, even in our modern world. Changing our beliefs and reframing our world also sends a message to our tribes. When I asked you what you might lose, this is what I was thinking. You can't change your mind if the net result is losing your community. You need somewhere to go to avoid isolation and loneliness. Joe, I will leave you with this one thought, and the only thing you need to remember: there is a world of color that you are ready to step into, and there is a world of people who want to join you."

Joe's eyes moistened at the thought.

Money and Value Loss

Issue: No client or student has ever come to the Mind Muscles Academy complaining that they weren't ready and eager for success and wealth. Instead, everyone assumes that they can step into wealth and be happy. However, as my clients approach the success they say they desire, they face unacknowledged losses. These unrecognized losses create a subconscious fear that sabotages their success time after time.

Exercise Description: This exercise presents a list of potential pain points attached to success, then queries beliefs about them.

Outcome: Discover any potential hidden losses that accompany your experience of wealth. Then create alternative beliefs and behaviors that mitigate any perceived loss.

Time to Complete: 30–60 minutes

Prerequisites: None

Exercise Access: You will find detailed instructions in your complimentary online course.

Join or log into your complimentary online course here:

https://conversations.money/book-exercises/

Chapter 30 — Who's Interviewing Whom?

Joe's phone vibrated, and he pulled it from his pocket while walking fast, holding a grocery bag, and avoiding a pile of trash heaped on the sidewalk. He traded hellos and brief small talk with Julie. Then she asked him how things were going with Maria Elena, his new editor.

"She asks hard questions, likes my ideas, and is paying me almost five times what my previous articles paid. I mean, it's almost as if I were a real professional!"

Joe could feel Julie's smile through the phone. "Oh my God, who knew?"

"It's still not a walk in the park. I need to do real research these next few weeks. It's so different. I can't just use the same old language that supported my old point of view. Every word is challenged and has to mean something."

"Well, if it were easy, everyone would do it. And don't worry about solving it all at once; just start. I've read that most productive people say their first efforts are usually awful."

"Are you saying the article's going to be awful?"

"Of course. But I'm there to criticize it, remember?"

"Teamwork!" Joe shouted, and they laughed together.

Joe climbed the stairs to his apartment, then spent a full minute wrestling with the key in the lock. It had been broken for at least six months, and the landlord showed no intention to fix it. When Joe finally stepped inside, it was clear the entire place no longer reflected who he was becoming. He opened the refurbished MacBook Air he'd recently bought and dove into urban apartment listings with gusto.

Despite feeling so good only a few moments ago, the prices for one-bedroom places in neighborhoods just this side of dangerous immediately burst his bubble. Pissed's voice came out of the blue and struck him forcefully, because he wasn't expecting it. "Landlords! They know you need to live somewhere, and they have you by the balls! You remember your article on rent control, don't you?"

Joe took a deep breath, a move that had become habitual at the first signs of stress. Yes, he remembered the article on rent control. If he played a little film called *Victim vs. Perpetrator* in his head, it all made sense. On the other hand, if he played a new feature called *Future Value*, he appreciated developers who risked their capital for long-term returns by creating living spaces for people, some of whom weren't even born yet.

Joe took another deep breath and said, "Gee, Pissed, you came on so strong that you surprised me."

"Don't you see that those goddamned capitalists are out to squeeze every living penny out of you?" Pissed shouted back. "What happened to fair housing prices? What happened to your concern for the poor?!"

"I can't solve all the problems in the world. And being angry about the problems that I can't solve keeps me stuck in this state of not accomplishing anything, even something small. I'm sorry, Pissed, but my beliefs, behaviors, and knowledge change when I play these new movies. This then shifts how I see the world.

I know there are structural barriers in our society, but I wonder how much of those barriers are absorbed and internalized? How much is changeable, and how much of those barriers are hard and fast in reality?"

Pissed remained silent.

Later that afternoon, Joe met with Dr. Bala Kironde, the founder of a controversial fast-growing charter school. The interview, which focused on building skills aimed at delivering value, went well—so well that it ran long.

Joe showed up later than expected at Julie's. Happy to see him, she opened the door and pulled him in with a hug and kiss. "How did it go?"

"Sorry I'm late. It got intense. There's so much I don't know that I don't even *know* what I don't know. But one thing is becoming clear: educational development is critical. Future skill sets will require a lot of very specific training, or else people won't be able to keep pace with technology. And if people don't even have the technology basics down, no matter what their career, they're going to get left behind."

"Let's talk about being left behind... but first, are you hungry? Chicken salad sandwich?"

"Really? Oh my God."

Julie grinned and opened the fridge.

While Joe ate, Julie listened with interest and asked clarifying questions. Joe talked about what he'd learned, as well as what he'd observed.

"We ran late and still didn't finish. We're meeting again next week."

"Yeah? So, what do you think the outcome is going to be?"

"We discussed a few possibilities. The article comes first, but Bala hinted at the possibility of me actually..."

"Actually... ?"

"Working with the school in some capacity. I mean, there was no offer or anything... just, you know, we tossed around a few ideas." Joe took the final bite of his sandwich, closed his eyes, and swallowed. "So," he said, "what can I do to repay you?"

"I'm a fiend for foot massages."

"I've never given one. But if there's a school, I'm all over it."

"You're in luck. It so happens I am the founder of Foot Massage Mentors. We mentor up-and-coming young men on how to give the best foot massage in the world."

"And how many people are in your organization?" As soon as he said the words, Joe realized he had taken her seriously for a moment. He felt a slight blush.

"Well, it's a very young organization."

"How young?"

"Two minutes."

"Well, I'm always happy to help up-and-coming entrepreneurs get a toehold... and a leg up... and step into a new business." He grinned as Julie groaned at the puns. "I would love to be your first student."

Chapter 31 — A Tale of Two Planets

Joe slowly set his clean dish in the drying rack, aware that he was not alone and Money's eyes were on him. Without turning around, he spoke at an even and unhurried pace. "I found a flaw in your thinking."

Money raised his eyebrows and leaned forward. The unexpected yet welcome guest sat at the kitchen table, patiently waiting for him to continue. Joe wiped his hands on a dish towel and dropped into the chair across from Money.

"Here's the flaw. You say that money is a Certificate of Appreciation because value is delivered on the recipient's terms. Is that correct?"

Money looked amused. "Joe, are you laying a trap for me? Look out—you may become Money!"

Joe grinned and continued. "Real funny. So, here's the problem you can't resolve with a reframe. You claim there is a higher moral value in delivering value to others. But what about the people who are unable to provide value? What about the mentally challenged, mentally ill, or people with a brain disease? What about people that are so disadvantaged that they don't have a chance at a good educa-tion? What about kids who grew up in abusive families? What about the unlucky ones struggling just to survive, looking in trash cans for their next meal?"

Money remained silent.

"You talk about delivering value to others, while there are people starving to death in the most horrible and gruesome circumstances who can't even feed their own children. How does your ethic of delivering value have any meaning for them? If you had this conversation with them, they'd think you're crazy."

Joe and Money remained silent while the wail of a passing siren filled the room.

"I don't have a solution for that, Joe."

"What? No magical reframe?" Joe paused, feeling desperate in the absence of a response from Money. "Here's a real-world issue that has nothing to do with my screwed-up beliefs or mindset, and you don't have a solution?"

"I imagine that's unsettling."

"Of course it's unsettling!" Joe's voice expressed irritation. "I bitch about something, and you patiently *invite* me to experience a different point of view. Many of these experiences, after a while, feel much better with this new frame of mind. But I still keep flipping back and forth between two very different worlds."

"As discussed, holding more than one worldview at the same time is real progress. In each context, we filter our experiences to allow in only the supportive stimuli. Not only is the information filtered, but the meaning we apply to that information is predetermined."

"What does this have to do with people struggling for their lives?"

"Let's create imaginary worlds as an exercise. Are you up for that?"

"Not if you're using it to avoid discussing the human problems you don't have an answer for."

"I promise I'll build a helpful foundation."

Joe pursed his lips before nodding.

"Remember, this is an exercise. You can keep anything or nothing. You said that the phrase 'at choice' was awkward. It is awkward because I want to create a new concept isn't muddied. Because you're 'at choice,' stepping into a new world is a riskless adventure. As you gain confidence in your moral self, your curiosity can expand without fear. It's like going to a foreign land and learning a new language."

"An imaginary world?" Joe smiled, thinking how much of his current life was "imaginary."

"Imagine that this new land is a parallel Earth-like planet in a different solar system. To get a sense of this new world, please just relax for a moment. In your mind's eye, I invite you to create a world very different from ours."

Joe leaned back, closed his eyes, and started to breathe deeply.

"Excellent. I see your breath getting easier and easier as this new planet comes into view. Notice how the geography has similar features to the earth. As we approach this planet from space, what do you see?"

"You want me to see something that doesn't exist?"

"Sure, like we're the directors of a new movie. As a writer, I'll bet you've had fantasies of a successful movie script."

"I've never told anyone about that! It's a dream most writers have."

"Great! Here's your opportunity to practice. What do you see as you come closer?"

"I see a planet, mostly blue. Clouds cover part of it. I see the polar ice caps. They don't have the air pollution that we do, and there's no global warming. I don't know why, but a large city in the center of a continent draws me in."

"Excellent. In your script, this planet evolved with very different cultures from our own. You can see this in their beliefs and behaviors."

"What beliefs and behaviors?"

"Let's start with an infant's experience from day one. On this planet, each baby is joyfully welcomed into this world. Babies are cuddled and loved. They see a world of adults smiling at them. The parents and adults in their lives read and sing to them from the day they're born.

"This is also a world of respect. From the first breath the baby takes, the parents and caretakers fully expect this child to grow into an adult that values their own freedom, and the freedom and independence of others. Every child experiences a community that consistently reinforces these cultural norms. Discovering themselves and the world is encouraged. Personal responsibility is internalized, just like gravity. For this reason, there are diverse educational programs available to all. Respect for the dignity and integrity of every individual is the foundation that drives the law, regulation, social agreements, taxation, economics, and personal rights and obligations.

"In this world, an act of violating someone else's boundaries is unthinkable. You might imagine on such a planet that there would be a substantial and enforced uniformity of culture. However, with the ethic of respect for individuality, many different types of cultures, societies, and religions have developed and thrived. Some of them are more individualistic, others more communal and collectivist. But one thing they all have in common is respect for each unique individual.

"Because most people are responsible and believe in voluntary relationships, their legal system is simple, and their laws have universal support. The basic laws prohibit violations of personal boundaries, such as murder, rape, assault, fraud, and broken contracts. Humans are still humans, and their flaws have not disappeared, but violations of the law stand out like a sharp knife on soft skin. When laws are broken, these violations are not tolerated.

"As far as economics go, central banks and governments do not direct the economy. Taxes are minimal and provide for a judicial system and law enforcement. The government provides infrastructure such as roads that would be difficult for private companies to develop. Most families have savings that can carry them through difficult times and support them in retirement.

"Because free-market competition provides continuous productivity growth without inflation, the benefits of this productivity flow to the citizens rather than being inflated away. Free-market competition is global, and free trade promotes international resource efficiency.

"In this scenario, there is very little poverty, because each person adds value to their community and receives value in return. Now, of course this planet isn't perfect. Some people don't add much value to their families and communities and would typically be poor. There are people with psychological issues, neurological and brain chemistry problems, and mental and social handicaps who sometimes have difficulty participating in value relationships. However, given the very high level of productivity overall, the amount of money required to help the needy is relatively small. Most charity is carried out through voluntary organizations that provide caring and training where needed, along with targeted welfare.

"Imagine this planet, Joe. Imagine how your experience of life would be different."

Joe slowly opened his eyes and blinked away the tears. He saw his dumpy apartment and felt something like an unexpected gut punch. "Money, what kind of utopia are you describing? This world is nonsense! You're describing a system where everything's working perfectly. You know this can't be real. And because it isn't real, you can't use it as an argument for anything."

"Yes, Joe, this may be a fantasy... or it could be a description of a planet from another star system where I also represent money. How appealing is this planet to you?"

"You create a perfect world, then ask me if I like it? You're joking, right?"

"If it is a joke, just humor me. We can learn something by working backward from this world."

Joe looked at Money quizzically.

"Yes, work backward. First, let's clarify all the factors that contribute to a wonderful world. Then we can see what pieces are missing in our current world. For example, we can see what contributes to physical, emotional, and financial well-being."

Joe's jaw tensed. "Humans aren't imperfect; they are *worse* than imperfect. You've created an impossible imaginary world so you can win a theoretical argument."

"I've created an imaginary world to give us clarity. Take a look at this imaginary world and see what elements you do and don't like. In this world, we have loving families, even nontraditional families. We have children that are cherished. We have parents that encourage their growth, skills, and education. Objections so far?"

Joe's brow wrinkled as he looked at the floor.

Money gave him a moment and then, with a tender voice, inquired, "What's happening right now?"

"I feel something pretty strong, but I'm not sure what it is."

"Allow the feeling to come forward and announce itself."

Joe's posture shifted as his muscles tensed. "I feel rebellious. Your world is a cult that demands conformity."

"You mean like your religious upbringing?"

"Somewhat."

"Were you pressured to conform?"

"Of course, but not nearly like I would be in your world."

"So the attributes you said were wonderful suddenly feel like pressure?"

"Yes. They pressure you to *be* wonderful all the time."

"Does this mean you want to raise your children without any values or ethics because it might feel like pressure? Raise them like wolves?"

"No, you have to raise children with values. But a part of me rebels against conformity."

"This is a most excellent point, because it brings up a critical distinction. From your rebellious point of view, this world feels like forced compliance that violates your freedom of choice."

"Bingo."

"Joe, are we brainwashing our kids, or are we inviting them to cultivate a mindset that produces a successful, happy life?"

"I don't know how to answer that."

"May I continue talking about the children on this other planet?"

"Sure."

"Children learn from an early age through modeling, stories, and adult behaviors, that meaning doesn't come attached to any outside phenomenon, but is created by them. For example, there are no expressions that mean 'that made me feel' or 'you made me feel.' Personal agency is baked into every part of the culture—their stories, heroes, history, education, and parenting. Every child knows that they are responsible for themselves, and everyone has an opportunity to build their own safety net, or in conjunction with family or community groups. These behaviors reduce the need for global bureaucratic welfare. As with the depression-era generation on Earth, the thought of being on welfare is repugnant.

"In your current world, most children of evangelicals become evangelicals, most children of Catholics become Catholics, and most children of Muslims become Muslims. Likewise, we can expect most children on this other planet to take on the mantle of personal agency and responsibility that all adults consistently model."

"So, it *is* brainwashing."

"Children in all cultures, good or bad, live in a context of the behaviors and beliefs that they absorb. This happens intentionally or unintentionally. So, the question is, how can we intentionally create a better world?"

"What makes your approach different from the postmodernist philosophy that rejects objective reality? It sounds like you believe our reality is shaped by our training and beliefs."

"Postmodernists are happy to supply meaning from a shifting base of race, culture, ideology, and society. In their world, there is no observable truth. Hence, everything is a social construct. I suggest we create meaning by developing our higher selves and a map of our world based on empirical testing, reason, and critical thinking."

"Those words have no practical meaning."

"From your current context, that is correct. However, I offer an invitation to open that door and create a new context."

"In your mythical world, what happens to the children who don't 'get it' and don't walk through that door?'"

"They'll find themselves out of step with the world around them, and find ways to survive or even thrive in a counterculture."

"Are you saying some people with moral failings will rebel and make bad choices?"

"No, I'm not condemning these people. Human complexity produces life complexity. So, Joe, what differences do you see between our world and this planet we created?"

"...*You* created."

"Yes, I created."

Joe closed his eyes to focus on the differences. "I suppose that deep down, humans are still humans. They'll still suffer. And neither world can totally relieve suffering."

"Indeed. The purpose of the exercise is to clarify our thinking. Next, let's clarify the legal system. The rule of law gives everyone a standardized way to build legal and commercial relationships."

"Money, if all laws are stable—or should I say 'stagnant'—culture would outgrow them quickly. The laws need to keep up with changing times."

"Yes, indeed. Everything is changing—and at the same time, principles don't. It's important to distinguish between laws, rules, and regulations that grow out of fundamental human values, and those that carve out selected advantages. If we can count on stable laws that prohibit violations of our human rights, we'll have the confidence to fully engage in long-term thinking, planning, and investing. Minimal and stable laws allow people to build value for the next generation.

"In this other world, it's a given that self-responsibility is a major cultural, familial, and religious tenet. Because of self-responsibility and legal compliance, taxation is minimal. Some of the countries in this world have a small sales tax. Others have small import and export taxes. One small country even taxes everybody the same amount, and then they get to keep everything they earn beyond that. But what they all have in common is keeping most of what you earn. You get to plan for the future, knowing that the rules of taxation and the rule of law are not going to shift out from under you. This confidence allows people to plan for the long-term generational growth of productive assets. In this world, the investment horizon can be as long as twenty, thirty, forty, or even fifty years."

"So, in this other world, what you're saying is that the rich get richer and the poor get poorer."

Money paused. "I'm glad you brought this up. There are certainly wide ranges of intelligence, motivation, skills, abilities, flexibility, creativity, and passion in this imaginary world. The luck of the draw also makes a difference. These differences create a wide range of ability to deliver value to others, which results in a wide range of wealth."

Joe folded his arms across his chest as Money continued.

"I can see that you're still skeptical of this process," Money said. "Remember, wealth is dependent upon delivering value. We can go into more detail about this imaginary world, but just from the highest level, does it look like a world that serves its people better?"

"Of course. But you are forgetting that humans aren't perfect, and there's still raw evil in the world."

"But is this other world a better place than ours?"

"Yes, I said that it was."

"In regard to this better world, we've discussed money peripherally, because it isn't even in a critical factor for well-being. Here's the punch line of this digression. *In our current world of suffering, poverty, struggle, and wealth differentials, the initial response is to blame the system.* In a world of complexity, humans look for simple solutions—and I'm an easy target. If you're focusing on only the symptoms, the obvious answer is financial redistribution. Redistribution not only feels good, but it has the benefit of allowing us to avoid the hard questions embedded in our cultural ethics and behaviors. Money as a measurement is the final financial stage of personal, cultural, political, and yes, even spiritual success or failure. But here is the real kicker: fixing the outcome and symptoms requires the threat or use of force to redistribute the money. Rather than increasing value with voluntary transactions and creating opportunities for everyone, the focus on financial outcomes does so without increasing the value we contribute to each other.

"Do you see what I'm getting at Joe? Money has little to do with poverty and suffering. Going back to our original conversation, giving everybody a wheelbarrow of gold won't improve the human experience. I daresay that even more fundamentally, the issue is spiritual. That is, spiritual in a generic sense. How meaning has evolved in a culture will impact people's motivation to deliver value. I've been around for thousands of years, and I've watched countless countries trying to solve symptoms with money. Not once in history has attacking the symptoms alleviated the problems of poverty and suffering. Not once."

Not long after Money left, Joe got a text from Julie. Peter and a few other people in their online community were going out that night to celebrate the opening of a new co-working space centered on the design arts, and she would be out for dinner. There was no implication that she wanted Joe to come along.

By late afternoon, Julie wasn't returning his texts, and a wave of self-doubt washed over him. As night darkened the city, Joe could hear Pissed stirring. Just how much fun was good old Julie having, anyway? *Obviously, too much fun to talk to you, Joe!*

At that moment, Joe realized he had a choice: he could spiral down into his familiar place, or step into his higher self.

He finished brushing his teeth and lay on top of the covers. He started with deep and slow breathing. With each breath in, he took in more air. With each breath out, he exhaled more air. While breathing, he did something that seemed counterintuitive: he told Pissed to scream louder. The juxtaposition of deep breathing and Pissed's voice was too much for him to handle, and Joe broke out laughing and sobbing at the same time. He crawled under the covers and fell asleep immediately.

Joe's phone pinged several times, bringing him back to the world of the living just before his alarm went off. It was a text from Julie.

Sorry about going AWOL. Great fun last night. Dinner at my place?

Joe took a deep breath and realized how susceptible he was to even little triggers that could create massive emotional earthquakes. The text should have fixed everything... but the pain was still there.

The bus ride to Julie's neighborhood brought some peace, as did the walk up 22nd Avenue to her apartment. Julie greeted him with a quick hug while talking on her cell phone. "Be done in a moment," she whispered to Joe.

Julie went into the kitchen and checked something in the oven, chatting away as she did. Joe sat down, checking email on his phone in a desperate attempt to keep himself occupied. Julie finally finished her call and stepped back into the room.

"I gotta keep checking the cake, so I'll be bouncing in and out. How was your day?"

"... Okay."

Julie was on her way into the kitchen, but turned around. "I feel a great disturbance in the Force, Luke. What's up?"

"Sorry. I'm okay."

Julie looked puzzled, but took her creation out of the oven and set it on the stovetop. "Joe, we agreed to be honest with each other. It doesn't take a sensate to feel this dark hole."

"Well, sorry, Obi-Wan."

Julie smiled in response. "I want to clear things up the moment they happen. Anything we bury becomes a growing time bomb."

"Is this where you say, 'man up'?"

Julie grinned. "If it fits, go for it."

Joe looked down at his shoes like an embarrassed little boy. "Well, I guess I was expecting something different from our relationship. You went out and had a good time, and then you didn't text me, and suddenly, I was afraid that..."

Julie sat next to Joe on the couch and took his hand. "It's okay, Joe. I'm afraid, too. Should you start, or should I start?"

"No, I'll man up." Joe managed an embarrassed smile, then described how much Julie meant to him already, and how any separation triggered fears of abandonment. He owned those feelings and said they had nothing to do with Julie. It was a well-worn repeated movie that played in his mind and was easily triggered. "I played out my fantasy of our relationship... Oh god, this is so embarrassing."

"I'd love to hear that fantasy. Is it sexy?"

Joe laughed louder than called for to cover the rush of feelings. "That would've been better. In my fantasy, we were just..."

"Just what?"

"Just us. I never saw you having fun with friends or other people or not letting me know what you're doing." Joe laughed again. "As I say this aloud, it sounds so childish."

"Whatever you feel is okay, Joe. Intense feelings are going to come and go, because real relationships never match fantasies. But thank you for the honesty. Once everything is on the table, then we can work through it together, as a team."

After sitting in the warm glow of silence for a few minutes, Julie spoke. "I have my demons, Joe. They're pretty powerful. They may be—no, *will* be challenging for you to handle. Some time ago, when I teased you and asked you to man up, there was more than just a tease there. I was testing you. I want to express myself honestly and have you stay with my extremes, so I feel safe in your strength."

"Julie, if I were to list all the people in the world with demons, you wouldn't even be on the list."

Healthy, Wealthy Family — Raise Yourself Again!

Issue: We are all imprinted with our family and cultural heritage. Our parents were driven by beliefs that we no longer hold, but which may still exist in our subconscious.

Exercise Description: You will clarify answers to some questions about your financial heritage and the heritage you would prefer to build on.

Outcome: You will build a foundation of your identity, beliefs, and behaviors that match your values and uniqueness.

Time to Complete: 30–60 minutes

Prerequisites: Read the chapter "A Tale of Two Planets"

Exercise Access: You will find detailed instructions in your complimentary online course.

Join or log into your complimentary online course here:
https://conversations.money/book-exercises/

Chapter 32 – Money and Meaning

"**I** cannot create meaning for you."

The voice came from behind Joe as he approached his apartment door.

"Did I ask you to?" Joe pushed the key into the worn-out lock, jiggling it until it turned. He opened the door without a glance over his shoulder.

Money followed him in. "But many people do. You did, too, at the beginning. By rejecting money, you created meaning by being righteous in your poverty. Others attach meaning to their lives by accumulating money for status and an ego prop. In both circumstances, money becomes a substitute for meaning."

"This feels like an admission, but you're right. Pushing money away allowed me to feel righteous, and that gave my life some meaning."

"Where do people traditionally find meaning?" Money asked.

Joe began to unload the bag of groceries he'd carried in. "Well, the obvious answer is religion and church. But fewer and fewer people are religious in the historical sense. I mean, many of my friends claim to be 'spiritual,' but it's more challenging to find any inherent larger meaning in that."

"Where else do people find meaning?"

"I suppose in family and community. Traditionally, in small towns, everyone had an extended family. You had grandparents, parents, uncles, aunts, and cousins. You were part of something that had solid history and values, where you belonged."

"And where else?"

"Although I haven't experienced it personally, it seems like patriotism and pride in national heritage could provide some meaning, but that is diminishing."

"And where else?"

"Geez... if we go way back, it's basic survival. You got up in the morning, you were hungry, and you needed to hunt or gather food. You needed your tribe to work together just to survive."

"So, Joe, where does that leave your generation?"

"The extended family is rare today. Our generation puts off marriage and children. Organized religious communities are shrinking. In our age of abundance, daily survival isn't an issue. And being patriotic is just embarrassing to many of us."

"Sports? Your team...?"

Joe grinned. "Yeah, it's come to that." He turned to the small window that was just beginning to collect dust again and allowed his thoughts to settle. "Affluence can't take the place of being part of something greater than ourselves. I read an article claiming people in affluent nations have more anxiety. You know, depression, drug use, suicide, divorce, alienation, loneliness... all the usual suspects."

"Suspects of what?"

"You're asking what drives these similar states? How about a deep longing for meaning that is evaporating?"

"If you frame money as Certificates of Appreciation, does that create the meaning you need?"

Joe pondered the question for some time. "It certainly removes the stigma from honestly acquired wealth, but it still doesn't contribute to real meaning or a greater sense of purpose. Before I met you, my map of the world attached a lot of meaning—or more accurately, *anti*-meaning—to money."

"And now?"

"Meaning as a human experience has nothing to do with money. If we conflate the two, we are setting up a problem that we can't solve. We will be stuck hating money or chasing it as a distraction from the harder question."

"That sounds like something I would say."

Joe stifled a smile. "That's embarrassing, but it feels right."

"And what is meaningful for you personally?"

Joe closed his eyes as his stomach tightened. He noticed the shift immediately and took several deep breaths. "I've cleaned up a lot of mental clutter, but nothing has replaced it. However, what has changed is the..." Joe paused.

"The what?"

"Maybe the courage or confidence to face uncertainty—you know, the unknown, and the confusion I feel when asking myself what *really* matters. In the past, it was so much easier to allow my friends— or at least the people I thought were cool and wanted as friends—it was easiest to adopt their values, so I wouldn't stand out or be ostracized. Writing as a 'social justice warrior' was, well, a way of being part of the pack. And being part of that movement is an easy way to feel meaning and that I matter. Probably not much different than belonging to a church. But looking back, if I were to do the three chairs exercise again, it would be different."

"How so?"

"The meaning of *meaning* has shifted."

"So, what is meaningful to Joe?"

"That isn't clear. *And,* it's okay that it isn't clear, at least for now. But I do know I prefer to have *meaning* evolve out of who I am and not some external group consensus."

"What will that do for your sense of community and belonging?"

"I don't know. But I see the light at the end of the tunnel. So, what if I have friends who have different beliefs? Like Julie. Julie's been a big part of the revelation that I am responsible for creating my world and my own life."

Money started to speak, then paused for a moment. "Are you aware of what you just said? Have you felt the power of this mindset? You are talking about your personal agency and the ability to define your own experience in the world. Everything changes when you assert dominion over your own life. Without accepting your own agency, the easy path is the slippery slope into victimhood. Without the experience of agency, life becomes a series of reactions to the meaning that has been assigned to you.

"Very powerful, to the point of being hard for me to hear. I feel like I am on a very high diving board excited and afraid to jump."

Money grinned. "Oh yes, how good it will feel when you let go and hit the soft water."

"Well, nothing is standing between myself and a meaningful life except me. I must admit, this new world feels terrifying. However, the train has left the station, and it isn't going back. Of course, there's a part of me that still says I'm not worthy, but I'm ready to acknowledge that voice, and at the same time step into a whole new world of worthiness."

"Is the worthiness shift sufficient?"

"When I claim my worthiness as a human being and my right to walk on this earth, everything changes. In this world, our many conversations about money and Certificates of Appreciation almost seem irrelevant. From this point of view, there is no need even to have those conversations."

Money raised his eyebrows and tilted his head.

"I create conflict with my mindset of feeling left out, let down, and treated unfairly. We worked through all those issues, and I fought all the way. But as I own my worthiness, those issues have no soil to grow in."

"So, could we have short-circuited our conversations by going directly to those mindset issues?"

"I don't know. But we're here, and it feels good."

Chapter 33 — From Depression to Delight

From: Joe Everie <JoeEverie@gmail.com>
To: Money <money@conversations.money>
Subject: Struggling with my next article

Dear Money,

I'm sitting in the canoe, writing an article that challenges my old economic beliefs. There is so much to say, and I am struggling. Thoughts?

—Joe

PS: You don't seem to come around as often.

From: Money <money@conversations.money>
To: Joe Everie <JoeEverie@gmail.com>
Subject: Re: Struggling with my next article

Dear Joe,

I have some terrible news and excellent news. I will be there later.

—Money

P.S. You are moving forward on your own. The beliefs that emerge from your personal struggle are far more helpful than the beliefs you adopt from others.

Joe read the email and returned to work.

A few hours later, he heard Money's voice behind him. "Is it too late to talk?"

Joe looked up from the laptop. "The timing is good. I'm still frustrated with the new article. But before we talk about that, you said you had bad news."

"And good news. Notice what you focused on."

"Yeah. That way, I'm braced for the kick in the gut and not blindsided."

"You're writing an article about improving educational outcomes. You want to communicate effectively. You want to invite your readers to adopt effective systems that will feel better and produce the outcomes they want."

Joe screwed his face up. "Okay, I'm finally sitting in the damn canoe. I'm writing about money as a Certificate of Appreciation. This article started with the simple task of describing Certificates of Appreciation and education, and skill-building to create value and financial stability. But I don't know how to stop explaining things so people can actually hear the message."

Money took a deep breath and placed a hand on Joe's shoulder. "Now you know how it feels to be me. I understand the frustration of explaining such a simple concept such as Certificates of Appreciation, and how it can trigger emotional reactions from different contexts."

"So, is that the bad news?"

"Yes. The good news is that you don't have to resolve the entirety of human nature with all its flaws. You don't have to improve the educational experience for all the children in the world. You don't have to change cultural norms about work ethic. You don't have to create meaningful lives for people who have lost their meaning in life. You don't have to create supportive structures and communities to help people through difficult times. You don't have to solve racism, sexism, or any other 'ism.' Joe, these issues are important, but you don't have to solve them all. If you place the burden of solving for human inadequacies on everything you write, you will never finish an article, let alone your book." Money relayed the words in his deep, rhythmic voice.

Joe leaned forward, took a quick SET score, and allowed his breathing to settle while digesting the impact of Money's words. Then he jerked his head up suddenly. "Yes. All or nothing."

"All or nothing?"

"Yes, when I wrote the article on the coming economic collapse, it was all or nothing. I needed to destroy the whole system for me to be okay. What you just said..."

Money maintained eye contact and settled in for Joe's response.

"I realize I'm in the same process of *all or nothing*. I have to have answers for everything. I'm pained by the size of the gap between what many people believe and these new sets of beliefs that, well, could work so much better for them."

"I honor your caring and your positive intention. From just the positive intention, where you didn't need answers for everything or to be responsible for all the suffering in the world, what would you prefer?"

"I don't know. But just thinking about the answer is a relief, because maybe..."

Money completed the thought. "Maybe you can start by caring about those in your community. Maybe your path is a road map for others who want to build rapport with their core values and their relationship with money. Maybe it won't even be a burden. Take it one step at a time and have fun!"

"Fun... ?"

"Your state of mind is critical. Pissed's voice only perpetuates your internal conflicts, and your readers will sense that. Do you remember the parable from the Bible about putting new wine into old wineskins?"

"But Money, I am so damn good at suffering!" Joe chuckled, amused by his self-deprecation.

"I'm looking forward to your next article. It could be the bare-bones outline of your book. Later, Joe."

"Later, Money."

Chapter 34 — Joe's New Job and Julie's Jab

"**W**hat do you mean, you have a job?" There was some irritation in Julie's voice.

Joe's head pulled back sharply. Julie responded automatically, touching his arm lightly. "Sorry. It's just such a surprise."

"When Bala made the offer, I was surprised, too," Joe said. "It's not a big salary, but it's still more than I've ever made in my life."

"That's great." Julie's countenance and voice were out of rapport, and Joe felt her coolness.

"I thought you'd be happy for me. What's up?"

"Nothing."

"Is this the same kind of 'nothing' you call me on?"

Julie turned her back and straightened a pillow on the couch. "Busted. Give me a minute to gather what's going on." She sat on the couch in silence for a long moment, then looked directly at Joe. "I want to establish a new rule. The rule is, you don't need to rescue or save me. You're not responsible for what I feel. I want us both to be aware of our feelings, accept them, and share them. Then we can look at them together while on the same team. That's what I want from you right now. Can you be with me and handle whatever comes up?"

Joe's new habit of taking a deep, slow breath kicked in, and he knew to remain silent.

Julie's tension lifted her off the couch, and she started pacing back and forth in the small room. "This is really funny. I told you not to saddle me, because my freedom is essential to me. And when you told me you had taken a new job that will radically alter your life, I realized that, oh my God, this could radically alter *my* life! Yeah. Until this moment, I haven't acknowledged that I was planning our life together. I know it doesn't make sense. I told you I need my freedom, then I turn around and feel hurt because you didn't discuss such a major life-changing decision with me."

Joe and Julie shared their physical sensations, feelings, and thoughts while they talked. They both paid attention to being defensive. Emotionally drained after an hour, they sat on Julie's couch, wrapped up in each other's arms.

Joe woke up on the couch under a blanket, with his head nestled in a pillow. The teapot was whistling loudly, and Julie was in the kitchen filled with morning sun. Joe quickly moved to the tiny bathroom. Julie had laid out towels and a new toothbrush. Her thoughtfulness brought a rush of gratitude.

"Do I smell breakfast?"

"Well, if it isn't Mr. Couch Surfer! You were dead out, so I put on the teapot to see if that would rouse you."

"Cruel, but effective." Joe sat down to share Julie's cheese omelet.

"I think you distracted me last night. We never did get into your job. Is this like an office job that's nine to five?"

"Hardly. There'll be meetings at the downtown charter school, but most of my work will be research, interviews, and arranging for publicity. I can do all that from anywhere."

"Do you have a clear mission?"

"Yes: to document the educational procedures and processes, compare the different methodologies, and evaluate what's most effective in each unique environment. Bala has a lot of experience and a pretty good framework for what works and what doesn't. So it's not like he's starting from scratch. He sees the future as dominated by technology and has the kids building web pages, learning to program, producing podcasts, even building solar collectors."

"That sounds wonderful. You get a steady income, and you still get to work independently and have a bigger mission."

" 'Bigger mission' is an understatement."

They both laughed. Joe got up and started clearing the table, as though this were an established habit between them. As he put the empty plates in the sink, a large envelope on the counter caught his eye. It was from the design school Julie had told him about all those weeks ago.

"More logos for your vision board?" he asked.

Julie shook her head. "That's an admissions application."

Joe gaped, at a loss for words.

"For the record, I wanted to talk to you about applying last night, but you stole my thunder."

"What happened? You stumble on a winning lottery ticket?"

"Something like that. I researched loan consolidation, and think I can pull this off in a way that makes sense. Plus, Peter is paying me a nice price—wow, say that three times fast—Peter is paying me a nice price for freelance work. I'll still need to work some hours at the deli, but I'll be doing the documentation work for some of his smaller projects."

Joe felt a rising wave of irritation. He put the envelope down and quickly went back to the dishes.

"Are you okay?" Julie asked.

"It sounds like you are going to be very busy."

"So you don't want me to apply?"

"Are you kidding? I'll write the essay for you if you want, if entrance essays are even still a thing. There's only one thing I'm asking for right now."

"And that is?"

Joe turned to Julie and looked her squarely in the eye. "Your word that if things

get too busy, you won't have a knee-jerk reaction and solve it by pushing me away first. If you do get too busy, we'll at least try to work it out. Can you agree to that?"

"Absolutely!"

Julie yipped as Joe picked her up and spun her around, knocking over a chair in the process.

Your Value "Vision Board"

Issue: Most of us focus on what we want. The problem is that these desires don't automatically put in place the process we need to achieve the desired results. Since vision boards are mostly about desired outcomes, we experience failure when the outcomes don't just magically happen. When everything else is in place except clarity around what we want, sometimes a vision board can supply that last break in the dam. So, this exercise is designed to put "everything else" in place.

Exercise Description: This exercise creates a vision board based on the value you will deliver to others. It asks you to determine what processes you can put in place that not only feel better, but get you to your goals.

Outcome: This clarification will plant the seeds for success in both your conscious and unconscious mind.

Time to Complete: About 1 hour

Prerequisites: None

Exercise Access: You will find detailed instructions in your complimentary online course.

Join or log into your complimentary online course here:*https://conversations.money/book-exercises/*

Chapter 35 — Conversation With Our Higher Self

J oe stared at the familiar yet slightly shifting face that Money had shown him over the last many months. Money maintained steady yet gentle eye contact.

"You're not really money, are you?" Joe said at last.

"What do you mean?"

"Exactly what I said. You really aren't money, are you?"

"You're right," Money replied.

Joe blinked to clear his eyes and bring Money back into focus. "So, who are you?"

"You know the answer to that."

"I'm on the verge of having the answer, but it won't quite come."

"Just stay with how it feels for the moment."

Joe closed his eyes for a couple of minutes and didn't say a word. Then, "Are you God?"

Money laughed gently.

"During our conversations, I've felt drawn to my higher self... to that self that represents the best me, and the best of what I want for myself and others."

"Well done, Joe."

"I'm not sure I understand."

"Yes, you do. You just said it."

"You mean the part about my higher self?"

Money remained silent.

Joe laughed nervously. "I see where this is going, and I'm not sure I can fully accept what I'm thinking."

"What are you thinking, Joe?"

"I'm thinking that you may have been channeling my higher self all along. But that doesn't make sense. I mean the emails, the 6:00 a.m. rise-and-shine visits..." Overwhelmed, Joe let his head fall into his hands. "I'm losing the ability to see you as *not me*," he muttered.

"Let's breathe together," Money suggested.

Their breathing gradually synchronized, slowly and fully. Finally, after a few minutes, Joe was able to release the feelings coming from his deepest place with a sob.

"Do you remember when you cried out for money, Joe? I came to you in the form of Money because, at that time, you had buried your higher self so deeply that it was the only way I knew how to start a conversation with you."

Joe rubbed the tears from his eyes, then stared at the chair where Money had been only a moment before. "I can't see you, Money."

"I'm still here," Money whispered.

"Where?"

"Here. I will always be here. We'll have some even more challenging issues to discuss as you impact the world." The sound was little more than the afternoon breeze blowing through the half-open window.

"It's okay," Joe said. "I am ready."

"Later, Joe." The words were so faint that Joe thought he might have imagined them.

He sighed and sat back in his chair, feeling for once that all was right with the world.

Epilogue

J ulie laughed so hard at the picture on Joe's phone that the other diners in the restaurant looked their way. The laughter was contagious, and soon Joe found himself laughing, too. "Samantha is always a step ahead of where I expect her to be. But then, just about the time I get used to her perceptiveness, she surprises me again," Joe said.

Julie smiled in a wave of gratitude sparked by the pride on Joe's face. Then she looked at the picture again. Samantha, their five-year-old daughter, had found a set of whiteboard markers and decorated her three-year-old brother's face with whiskers.

Joe whispered as if telling a secret. "She said she needed a lion for her zoo and enlisted Nathan."

Julie put her hand to her mouth to hold in the tenderness she felt before she could respond with a vivid memory. "Ten years ago to the day, the wind blew our wedding away."

Joe shook his head, picturing Julie's mom running for the pavilion when the unexpected squall had blown in from the Pacific.

"Nobody will ever forget our wedding, that's for sure..." Julie's voice trailed off as she recalled the awkward guy who always asked for chicken salad on rye. The path to this moment together had been challenging. They had been through a miscarriage, her parents' death, and the loss of her first business. She felt her eyes moisten as her hands reached across the table and rested in Joe's open palms.

Joe allowed the moment to just be before responding. "Ten years ago, I wasn't sure who I was in the world. But, boy, did you take a big chance when you said 'yes.' "

Julie grinned. "Oh, it was kinda like buying an undervalued stock because the analysts had missed the real value."

"I'm reduced to a market metaphor?"

"You were an investment—but a long-term-value one. So far, the two dividend payments have been fantastic."

They both laughed softly.

"How did the meeting with the committee go?" she asked.

"Well, the final pieces are in place. We got the go-ahead for the building, the financing, and all the permits and approvals for the second school. Of course, the teachers' unions weren't happy and will do their best to make us look bad, but we have about two hundred parents asking to be on a waitlist, and we haven't even made a public announcement! Not only that, but we have inquiries from many other cities."

"Joe! I had no idea you were that close. May I give you an appreciation?"

Joe had taught this technique to Julie over a decade ago, and it was now one of her signature tools. "Only if you must," he said playfully.

"You've created a path for challenged kids to have a better life. Since Bala's death, you have carried on and made the schoolwork for the parents and the kids. Your core beliefs about personal worthiness, setting boundaries, and delivering value have inspired the kids to learn and become skillful. When I visit a class, the teachers have created magic that balances structure and freedom. It feels so good to see self-motivated and excited kids solve their problems on their own or in groups. And your funny stories about Money in your courses on career, savings, and finances have been such a hit that they made the national news."

"Well, with a bit of luck... Having Pedro make a million dollars on YouTube at sixteen years old and giving the school so much credit kind of put us on the map."

"It's not just Pedro. That may have been luck, but it isn't luck that dozens of kids doomed to poverty are now ambassadors for the school and starting college. That means so much. Joe, remember that first article you wrote about capitalism?"

"Yes." Joe paused, trying to remember that world. "I was too angry to realize that I don't have to solve the world's problems. Instead, I can develop the skills and talents to impact those around me. And if everyone..."

"Yes, your book has encouraged parents to raise their kids with an appreciation for delivering value to others and feeling the pleasure of receiving Certificates of Appreciation—kids who are eager to deliver value and even enjoy their wealth!"

With magical timing, the waiter set down two glasses of red wine. Joe and Julie picked them up and held eye contact for a long moment filled with a decade of love and gratitude. Then they lightly touched glasses, the *clink* sounding like a bell, and toasted the next ten years.

Your Relationship with Money — Three Chairs Exercise

Issue: What has changed? What beliefs and behaviors have shifted since the start of this book and the online course?

Exercise Description: Repeat the Three Chairs Exercise that you completed earlier in the book. Now compare the three voices that speak for different parts of yourself.

Outcome: Has anything shifted? If so, on what level do you notice the change? For example, have your behaviors become more effective? Have your beliefs about the world created more opportunities? Have you noticed any changes in how you see yourself in relation to money and adding value to the world?

Time to Complete: 30–60 minutes

Prerequisites: Completing all the exercises in your online course

Exercise Access: You will find detailed instructions in your complimentary online course.

Join or log into your complimentary online course here:
https://conversations.money/book-exercises/

Additional Support for a Money-Positive Life

N ow that you have completed the book and the exercises in your free online course, you have created a new path for yourself. For some readers, this path may be brand new, and hold some fears and uncertainties. For other readers, this book and the exercises may have confirmed and clarified their core values and what they want for their well-being.

Creating new beliefs and behaviors, even those that serve us better, can feel unsettling at first. As Joe discovered, there are internal parts of himself that voices keeping him locked in a relationship with money that did not serve him well. As he and Julie built a family and business, they continued challenging the beliefs and behaviors that didn't fit their mission and highest values.

Just like human relationships, our relationship with money is ever growing and expanding. I have coached very successful professional money managers who discover new issues as they hit major wealth targets.

If you feel satisfied with this story and the exercises for now, please remember the Golden Keys. Enjoy your self-awareness, accept what you discover with curiosity, and ask the question from that foundation: "So, what do I want now?" As you proceed down this path to a Money-Positive life, we are here to support you now and in the future with the following resources:

- Money Academy Online Course — your self-directed money-positive path
- Wealth Workshops — live online meetings and group support
- Money-Positive Community — create connections, friends, and support
- Money Metrics — measure what matters
- Private Coaching — personal target support

You can find these resources at https://conversations.money/

Appendix — Major Principles: Review and Summary

T his review is a pithy description of some of the major models that *Conversations with Money* is built upon. It is written for readers who would like a quick review after reading the book, and for those that just want to see the major assertions. If any of these concepts trigger a negative reaction or a counterargument, great! You can refer back to Joe's struggle with the issue, take our online course, or join one of our live online meetings or groups to gain clarity.

Agency — The Power of Personal Ownership

Agency is the ability to create our own experience in the world. Everything changes when we assert dominion over our own lives. Without this belief, the easy path is the slippery slope into victimhood. Without the experience of agency, life becomes a series of habitual reactions and dealing with the consequences of impulsive behaviors. The power of agency can reach into our remembered past by helping us reframe our memories to give us a more robust experience in the present. In real time, we can be the author of the meaning we apply to our life encounters. With agency, we can imagine a better future—and step into it with confidence.

What matters? Do your experiences act on you, or do you act on your experiences? Does the experience itself matter, or is it the meaning you assign to your experience? What is the source of the meaning of your experience? When we ask the question this way, we have now asked the right question. It becomes obvious that the experience itself can't determine the meaning. We are left with the conclusion, desired or not, that we have agency, and we determine the meaning of our own experiences.

Once we use this model, a new powerful position in the world is available. The outside world no longer determines our experience. But this model also demands responsibility from us if we are the agents of our own experience.

Agency creation starts with real-time awareness. As we observe our internal state and our reactions any quickly triggered behavioral circuit can be rerouted through the executive function of our prefrontal cortex. We are then able to complete the circuit from the perspective of our higher-level self. The more we experience the power of agency, the more competent we are and the more ability we have to expand this power.

How can you take advantage of the power of agency? You can deliberately shape your world. This is an intentional state of being and can be expanded with practice. Start small with an experience you don't like. Take ownership of it and list all the potential meanings that a variety of people could possibly assign to that event or experience. Notice your patterns of interpretation. What other meanings would you prefer to assign to this experience?

Become the creator of your life.

Awareness and Acceptance — SET Development

Self-awareness is where we start. Self-awareness is the foundation for a life that is in rapport with ourselves, others, and the world. If we aren't aware of ourselves in real time, then our options and choices become automated reflexes, repeating old patterns of behavior that no longer serve us. There are many Eastern and Western traditions for expanding our real-time self-awareness. The Mind Muscles Academy model is the SET Awareness Workout. This is a step-by-step exercise that allows you to start where there is no clear beginning.

Self-awareness is free. Building your personal awareness is available to everybody at every stage of success. You know for certain that if you go to the gym and consistently work out with weights under the instruction of a trainer, in a few months, your body will have reshaped itself. Your mind can accomplish the same thing! We used to think that our brains were fixed, but neuroscientists now know that your brain is continuously shaped by our behaviors and beliefs. They call this reshaping process "neuroplasticity." Everyone can build new "Mind Muscles" that are designed to expand their personal awareness.

We break down our awareness into three different areas of focus:
1. Sensations (physical)
2. Emotions (feelings)
3. Thoughts (quality)

You can start by simply setting an alarm to ring every thirty minutes or at comfortable intervals. When it goes off, just notice your physical sensations. Take a slow trip from your nose to your toes. What do you notice? Leave the sensations as they are, without adjustment. Also, notice any judgments or self-criticism of what you discover, and let them come and go. Now journal about what you notice, without changing anything. Keep the alarm set, and keep the journal up to date. Soon this will become a very interesting habit.

Once this becomes easy, repeat the process, only this time, notice your feelings or emotions. No judgments, just awareness. Keep the alarm ringing and the journal up to date.

Once you've got this down, move on to the next step: your thoughts. When the alarm goes off, notice the quality of your thoughts. Are they negative or positive? Are they judgmental or kind? Are you lost in the flow of work or pleasure? Are you retelling yourself a story of hurt or unfairness? Are you playing a mental movie to justify what happened to you? Again, just notice; no changes are needed.

Once this becomes routine, you can run through all three aspects of awareness at the same time: your sensations, emotions, and thoughts. Again, no judgments, just curiosity, and awareness.

When you have accumulated plenty of information, review your journal. What do you notice? What patterns emerge? What is helpful? What no longer serves you? Now you can ask, "What do I prefer instead?"

Beliefs and the Power of Tribes

New beliefs impact our human connections. Upgrading our beliefs to those that serve us better creates tremors throughout the rest of our lives. One such major shake-up is our sense of belonging. Humans are tribal creatures, even in our modern world. Changing our beliefs and reframing our world changes how we relate to our current communities and can threaten our sense of belonging. Humans resist change, even change for the better, if they fear losing their community and the resulting isolation.

This risk and cost can be mitigated.

The first strategy for mitigation is acceptance. You can accept the beliefs of your current community, just as you accept yourself and the previous beliefs you held. You can think of beliefs as models that work more or work less. Without the need to hold onto previous beliefs as part of a survival mechanism, you no longer need to be defensive. This self-confidence will allow you to be part of many communities that have a wide variety of models for themselves and the world.

The second strategy for mitigation is the availability of supportive new communities. With new beliefs, your openness to the world will reveal new relationships and communities that enhance your new models and beliefs. This will allow you to step into a new world that supports refinement of and improvement on the new models you have developed for yourself, providing the opportunity for more honest, open, and supportive relationships and even new friendships.

Your imagined loss becomes a gain. With these two strategies in mind, your more primitive survival mechanism will be able to incorporate new beliefs and models without fear of isolation and loneliness.

Capital — The Excellence of Excess

Excess capital can be invested in our future. Humans' ability to invest in the future for our children, grandchildren, and our world is directly correlated to the amount of capital accumulation. If everyone had just twenty dollars in their pockets, we would all be focused on finding water and food. As we accumulate more capital, our focus stretches into the future. There are many examples of very wealthy people who invest in very long-term projects that governments just aren't structured to tackle, because of the short-term self-interest and risk aversion of politicians and bureaucrats.

Wealth redistribution is like killing the cow for the meat and depriving the yet-to-be-born children of milk. Once the wealth is distributed, investments in new technology, infrastructure, medical advances, farming, and human well-being are reduced.

Certificates of Appreciation

Money is appreciation. If you give me something that I value, I give you my Certificates of Appreciation. Whatever you give me, be it food, housing, entertainment, travel, or knowledge, I value your contribution. I appreciate it so much that I give you Certificates of Appreciation in return. I may also give you a verbal or written acknowledgment of my appreciation with a "thank you."

Wealth contributes to well-being. If I create value for you and many others, I can collect a lot of Certificates of Appreciation. In fact, with honest products and services, the more Certificates I collect, the more value I have delivered. Wealth that comes from value delivered is one measure of contribution to the well-being of my community and even the world. This then supports more capital accumulation. (See "Capital — The Excellence of Excess.")

Context — The Context We Choose Creates the Life We Live

The context we select determines everything. The context we live in filters the information we receive, feeds our biases, creates our truth, and sets our direction.

Context becomes an internalized system protected by a bubble that defends itself at all costs.

I know how to behave in different contexts. When I walk into a church, I step into that context. I know all the rituals, hymns, beliefs, and language. When I walk into a bar celebrating a sports team victory, I know the rituals, cheers, beliefs, and language. When I am in a transformational group, my body language shifts, and I use appropriate eye contact, touch, tone of voice, and language.

The context is consistent. Now, imagine a context that incorporates our identity, beliefs, behaviors, skills, and knowledge. Everything in this system is coherent. We are safe in this context, and indeed, we surround ourselves with others who share the same context. We know we share the same context because we use the same language, which does not need to be challenged or examined. Our thinking fits the context without rigorous examination.

The context creates the struggle. When I am in the context of dieting, I struggle every moment of the day to avoid eating the whole pizza. Within that context, change, even for the better, is a struggle requiring discipline. When I step into the context of a healthy self, there is no struggle within that context. I can feel the hunger, but it reminds me of my power to be strong and make healthy choices.

Struggle can be defined as pushing against a new belief or behavior from within a context that is defending itself from intrusion. **So, how do we step into a new context that serves us better?**

First, we expand our awareness of our current context. Define it clearly, including not only our internal mindset, but our external family, community, language, beliefs, and behaviors.

Once we have accepted it and labeled it as a context, then we can look at it from our higher and wiser selves.

Practice stepping into and out of a context intentionally. What is that like? What shifts as you step from one context to another? What mindset is needed to wear a context like you wear your clothes? This practice increases our awareness of each context and its details.

Next, accept each context as it is. Even if a context no longer serves you, at one point it did. Each context has an underlying positive intention. What is that positive intention?

Finally, with awareness and acceptance, you can now ask... *"What context do I want to create that serves me better?"*

Core Value: Respect for the Dignity and Integrity of All

This means I respect how everyone chooses to live their lives. For all our imperfections as humans, each person has the right to be an agent of their own life.

We are deeply flawed as humans. Yes, as humans we are still on a long path to engage our higher self. Given our biology and our evolutionary brain structure, our progress will be unsteady. We have come a long way since the dominance of our "lizard brains."

Given our flaws, where does agency reside? Allowing each person to have the autonomy to learn and grow is the best way to keep our flaws from metastasizing. If the same flawed people are managing other's lives through political force, then our individual flaws are magnified.

Dignity is a way of respecting people, not just by allowing them to be, but by honoring them and their choices. In my current model, everyone is selecting the best choices they have on their menu. My value invites everyone to expand their personal life menu to include choices that serve them and their world better.

Integrity can be defined in an engineering sense, as in the integrity of a bridge. As a result, I will not confer on a government or political force the ability to remove an individual's right to structure their lives the way they see fit.

This value is reciprocal, as I am of value as a human. I expect others to respect my own dignity and integrity. If they choose not to respect my value as a human being, then I will set boundaries. If they violate my clear boundaries, then they have expressed their own values. I will play the game by their rules as a way of defending myself in the safest and most minimal way possible.

What if everyone was able to live this core value? If so, most of the problems we experience psychologically, socially, culturally, and politically would largely disappear. Trying to fix the "symptoms" of human suffering without addressing the underlying philosophical, psychological, spiritual, social, and cultural context creates even more unintended consequences. The more issues that are fought on a symptomatic basis, the more the underlying problem pops up elsewhere.

Our work as humans is to continuously develop our own mindset that allows us to respect the dignity and integrity of every person.

Economic Mobility — Expanding Life's Menu for All

Our brains want to create permanent classifications. When we think of a group of humans as a class, race, culture, ethnicity, or religion, it allows our brains to make heuristics or mental shortcuts. Our brains want to reduce infinite potential complex calculations by creating simple classifications that assume fixed limitations.

Individuals move up and down the economic ladder. Some studies of economic mobility show much greater advances and downward slides on the economic ladder than most of us would guess. What if the people in our collective classifications, including those in our own classification, believe in the limitations that we ascribe to that group? What is the result?

On the other hand, what if we didn't create those limitations? What if we all believed that economic mobility and greater life choices are available to all? What if all children from all communities were taught the mindset and context of each economic strata? Each child as they grew could make the trade-offs and choices in education, training, work ethic and risk. What if our news, media, education, advertising, and games all supported the skill expanding our life choices?

Equity and Power

Clan discipline is enforced by direct personal relationships. Once a clan grows beyond a small amount (some say that it is a maximum of fifty people), the social cohesion maintained by direct relationships starts to break down and is replaced by hierarchical power structures. These power structures arise in all human societies.

A utopia requires enforcement. A utopian vision of equal outcomes must overcome the nature of man, all his animal hard wiring, and the hierarchical process of nature itself. This requires a lot of attention and energy, because no matter what the vision promotes, it still needs to account for humans as they are. If it promotes equality of outcome, it also requires a tremendous amount of power. Without power to enforce the vision, equality shifts back to a normal distribution of wealth. Once the power is established to mandate equality of outcome, then you have established inequality of power. Some have it, some don't.

Capitalism isn't a competition for wealth or money. Capitalism is a competition to deliver value on the terms of the recipients. Now, given the human condition of longing for love and trying to fill that hole in their hearts with anything but, often money and the chase for money is substituted.

Which condition would you rather live under? Would you prefer to live within a range of economic disparity, or would you prefer to live under a power disparity?

Golden Keys

Positive change starts with the Golden Keys. The Mind Muscles model for creating new behaviors that serve us better is the Golden Keys. For too long, most of us have tried to make changes through discipline, willpower, and control to motivate ourselves to adopt better habits or behaviors. Like many New Year's resolutions, our good intentions don't produce the results we want. We just keep repeating the same unwanted behaviors over and over again, with the same results.

Why do you do what you do? Have you ever looked at a previous day's behaviors and wondered why you did something? Does it almost seem like someone else might have taken over your body? Do you swear you will never repeat that mistake ever again—then a week later, experience pain from repeating that same behavior? The Golden Keys are all about creating new behaviors that serve us better.

The Golden Keys are as follows:

1   Awareness in real time

2   Acceptance of what we discover

3   Asking "What do I want now?"

Awareness is the first Golden Key for a reason. Once we have an awareness of *how* we create our current behaviors that produce our current results, then we have the ability to change the method we employ so we can create what we really want.

The next key is Acceptance. If there is one word that describes our work at the Mind Muscles Academy, it is *rapport*. If we are constantly fighting ourselves and our world, we do not have the ability to dance with our environment. After we become aware of our current processes, next we accept what we discover without judgment.

Become an expert on yourself! You can be like an anthropologist studying yourself with curiosity and wonder. You can love every part of yourself. This is a big step for many of us, and an important one as well.

Asking "What do I want now?" Built on the foundation of awareness and acceptance, we have a new foundation to uncover what we want instead. With the acceptance of what we discover, we no longer need to fight ourselves. Asking what we want now is not from the place of struggle, but from the place of discovery and adventure.

Government and Money Rules

The rules for a civil society that Joe and Money settled on are as follows:

1. All monetary transactions are voluntary and exclude the use or threat of force.

2. All transactions are transparent and honest.

3. Each individual determines the value of every transaction for themselves.

Governments violate all three rules. If you give this a moment's thought, you will realize that all three rules Joe and Money devised are totally always violated by all governments throughout history, and this is unlikely to change.

All governments threaten or use force to ensure compliance. Try not paying your taxes, and you will experience force. Resist, and you will be physically subdued or killed. Sounds dramatic, but imagine ignoring all rules and then resisting law enforcement. Even though this isn't part of our conscious thinking, we know it to be true, and we act accordingly.

So, how do we apply these rules to the government? In our model, almost everyone wants to live in an orderly society that has a rule of law, equality under the law, and enforcement of the law. Few people advocate anarchism or want to live in that world. Every day, we implicitly agree to the rules by obeying them.

The level of restrictions that is best for any country will vary widely. We have seen examples of the success and wealth in Hong Kong with a minimal government after the devastation of WWII. The British established a rule of law with minimal interference that allowed its citizens to transform a rock in the ocean, with no natural resources, to a wealthy society. We understand what it's like to live in either North Korea or South Korea today. If we recognize both the value of these rules and people's need for some consistent economic structure and process, then we can ask the right question:

How can we apply these rules to every governmental structure as completely as possible?

1. How much process can we move from the force of government to the cooperation of civil society?

2. How can we best create a government process that is transparent and honest?

3. How can we give each citizen as much agency as possible over their own lives and allow them to determine their own values and what is of value?

4. How do we measure the cost of violating these rules against the benefit?

By asking these questions, we will come up with a world of creative cooperation.

Maps and Territory

Certainty about absolute truth is fragile. What you believed about the world when you were young is different from what you believe now, and it will be different from what you believe in the future. If you think you hold the absolute truth at any point in time, then you need to shut out all information that doesn't support the truth. This requires a fixed mindset that is out of rapport with reality. Just like tectonic plates that shift, building tension that ends in an earthquake, holding fast to beliefs sets up a major tension that sets you up for personal disruption. You can move gently with your openness to your experiences, or experience major disruption in your life when the big one hits.

Alfred Korzybski famously said that "The map is not the territory."

What if you were to look at your beliefs as an imperfect map of reality? What if your job were to continually update the map with feedback from your journey? I teach my clients to add this to their communication.

- "My current way of thinking is..."
- "The model I am using for this problem is..."
- "I am currently looking from the framework of..."
- "I found a filter that really works well right now."

Defending a current "absolute truth" is a burden. Holding what you know as an imperfect map relieves all of us of the burden of defending an absolute truth. It opens the door to wider views of the "territory" that provide valuable feedback. It allows for incremental improvements in our map of how we operate in the world and avoids that big belief earthquake.

How do our maps and models work? Reality is persistent and will give us the feedback we need to constantly upgrade our beliefs and behaviors. It is a great feeling and experience the results our time-tested maps of the world and create modifications that continually serve us better.

Meaning — Where is It Located?

Where does meaning come from? Does meaning come attached, a priori, with the event or experience? Or are you the agent and creator who decides to choose the meaning of what you experience? Both worldviews offer a very different context to live your life and your ability to create rapport and harmony with your community and the physical environment.

Do you need to protect yourself from the world? If meaning is attached to the event, then our response is either shielding ourselves from unpleasant events, or trying to change the world to create a better experience for ourselves. The extremes of this model are expressed in "microaggressions." With microaggressions, the "aggressors" need to be reeducated to create a safer world for ourselves. In other words, the aggressor creates meaning for us. This is a position of powerlessness.

We have the power to create the meaning we want. If meaning resides with us, then any perceived aggressors lose their power. This is because we determine our own values, and we have every right to walk on the earth with our shoulders back and our head held high. We create the meaning of what is said to us. We stop looking for microaggressions, and the world stops delivering them, because we are in charge of the meaning.

Mistakes

She is three and exploring her world. Imagine a three-year-old child exploring the world and learning about gravity. She falls down a slippery slope. Do you berate her for making a mistake? She can't learn about gravity or friction without experiencing how she interacts with these forces. Is that learning experience a mistake?

Do you berate yourself? Now, as an adult, you have experienced some negative consequences in your own life. What does our internal judge say? "You made a MISTAKE!" For many of us, this brings feelings of guilt or even deeper shame. Some of us felt traumatized by early reprimands, so to keep ourselves "safe," we avoid taking risks, lie about our mistakes, defend ourselves, or even harbor feelings of unworthiness.

What if mistakes didn't reflect the value of our own worthiness? What if we didn't need to be defensive? What if we corrected or fixed any negative impact we had on others as part of our learning process? How would this change our life's trajectory?

What if mistakes were simply *feedback*?

Money and Acid

What happens if a human being loses all sense of meaning in life? Each of you can answer that question for yourself. For most of our clients, meaning is foundational for a happy, productive life. We know that those who suffer from depression often feel that life is hopeless and without meaning.

Our model for a fulfilled life includes delivering value to others. This bonding, connection, feedback, and community satisfaction are meaningful to many. For some, this is a spiritual value that transcends temporary pleasure. If money is a Certificate of Appreciation, then the more money you make, the more value you deliver, the more satisfaction you feel about your life. Think about the power of money in this context.

Now, let's look at gaining money without delivering value. Ask yourself, on some level—even a subconscious level—does the person who gets this money recognize that they are receiving value without delivering value? How does this impact their identity? How does this impact their feeling of worth? How does this impact their behaviors?

In our model, receiving value without delivering value is acid to the soul. It cuts us off from a loving connection to our communities. Humans are designed to be connected. This disconnect can impact not only individuals, but communities and nations as well.

Money-Positive Life

A money-positive life accepts money as part of life and a measure of value delivered. Money and wealth are accepted as markers for a broader positive life. Because money is a result of delivering value to others, it loses its emotional focus and is not needed to fill empty holes in our hearts. Because it reflects our ethic of respect for the dignity and integrity of every individual, it brings a deep satisfaction as a reflection of the meaning we have created.

Money Rules

The rules that Joe and Money settled on are as follows:

1. All monetary transactions are voluntary and exclude the use or threat of force.

2. All transactions are transparent and honest.

3. Each individual determines the value of every transaction for themselves.

Imagine, just imagine, that everyone on the planet internalized these rules. Create an imaginary world where all its citizens internalize and operate under these rules. How would government shift? What would happen to the economy? How would the time frame for planning, investing, and thinking change? What would happen to military conflicts? How would international trade be affected?

Imagine how this would impact every aspect of your own life, your family's well-being, and the communities that matter to you.

Process, Not Outcome

Our brains are programmed to want outcomes. Many vision boards are about outcomes. They capture the fancy car, the chalet in the mountains, an attractive mate, or exotic vacations. Most of us have dreams about the lifestyle and possessions that we desire. For those whose focus is caring about the world, we desire equality, justice, and fairness.

These outcomes become our dreams. Depending on how we go about getting the desired outcome, we can either experience continual failure, or pride in what we have accomplished.

The difference? Process over outcome. Focusing on a desired outcome without giving any thought to the process of achieving it = discouragement and hopelessness.

What processes support the outcome we want? As we improve our process, that is a victory in and of itself. We can get feedback from the process and continually improve it. Repeated processes become habits that are even more easily repeated as they become part of our lives. Once we establish a process for one outcome, get feedback, and then improve the processes, we become experts in process creation and integration in our lives. Once we have this ability, our life changes from one of discouragement to one of agency and power.

Victim and Perpetrator

How do you filter your world? There are many ways to filter and create meaning in a complex world full of layers of relationships. One filter is to look at the world through the eyes of victims and perpetrators. Yes, there are real victims who have suffered the most unimaginable pain and death at the hands of real perpetrators. There are evil people who have lost their humanity and violate even the most innocent. Having mental preparation, boundaries, and skills to meet or avoid these psychopathic individuals and groups can help.

What is the impact of labeling ourselves and others as "victims"? Even when the label is somewhat valid, it implies reduced agency. (See "Agency — The Power of Personal Ownership.") Our human brains grab onto victimhood as a righteous position. When we integrate the label of "victim," it is more challenging to take responsibility for ourselves. It is more challenging to create environments where we can expand our choices. It is more challenging to get excited about the future and feel optimistic and hopeful. The victim mindset filters for and even creates a world of injustice, filled with victims and perpetrators.

We lose agency. Victimhood becomes our identity and defines our beliefs and our behaviors. We attract people who are using a similar model, and they become our community. Soon, all hope depends on others organizing our environment so that we are safe.

Wealth and Value Contribution

It is nobler to be poor than to be rich and lose our soul. This is the subconscious belief that many clients bring to our work. Although the belief is subconscious, it still drives much of their other beliefs and behaviors—or better stated, it limits their experience of the world.

Imagine two very different sets of friends.

One set eschews wealth and prefers to experience life fully and richly. They love parties, sex, and getting high. They believe learning complex skills is giving into the power structure. Life is about love, not competition. Greedy capitalists have more than their fair share of the wealth, and most of their income should be taxed. In this group, their income is hand-to-mouth, and there are no savings for unexpected expenses or retirement. They move in and out of various social welfare programs.

What about the second set of friends? They also party and have a good time, but their focus and satisfaction center around creating a future for themselves and gaining the knowledge, skills, and behaviors that can deliver extraordinary value to others. They read a wide range of books and focus on their education to develop their talents. As they become adults, they build bridges, research medical cures, start technology companies, and deliver a tremendous amount of value to their communities and the wider world.

The second set of friends become extraordinarily wealthy. How much value has the first set of friends contributed to you? What about the second?

This next concept may boggle your mind:

The wealthier you are, the more value you have delivered.

Yes, there is fraud, cheating, con artists, and thievery. We know there are lottery winners and trust fund babies. But they are a small part of the whole.

Yes, there are spiritual values that trump everything. There are people who deliver huge cultural value without making any money, such as Martin Luther King, Jr., Mother Teresa, and Gandhi. You don't have to be one or the other... but do you know how you are best suited to deliver value? Either choice is okay.

If the primary value you deliver is commercial, does your bank account reflect the value you deliver to others? If not, can you increase the value you deliver? Can you get compensated for that value? Are you worthy of being paid for the value you deliver? Will your net worth reflect the increasing value delivered in ten years? What skills do you need to get paid for the value you deliver?

Notice your experience as you step into wealth as a positive value.

Zero-Sum Game — One-Pie Economy

There is only so much money, and it isn't theirs. This was said of the wealthy from a well-known figure. This is also a rally cry for many. There is only so much to go around, they say, and it just isn't fair that so few have so much and so many have so little.

Wealth is the end product of creating value for others. Yes, there are people who use force, fraud, and unethical behavior to gain wealth. But in a free market with a rule of law, most wealth is the product of value creation. Yes, at any given point in time, there is only so much currency. However, there is no limitation on the value we can create. So, the number of currently available dollar bills isn't what matters. It is the creative mindset that makes the difference.

What matters is how much value we are creating for each other. That value is almost infinite. As we leverage our intelligence, become more productive, and have the capacity to customize the value on an individual level, we will be able to deliver more value every year. Rather than worrying about the distribution of dollar bills, what if we focused on how we can all create more value for each other? How would the world be different?

CPSIA information can be obtained
at www.ICGtesting.com
Printed in the USA
BVHW051106091221
623632BV00008B/334